COURTHOUSE CHAOS

COURTHOUSE CHAOS

Famous & Infamous Trials, Mob Violence, & Justice

Andrew E. Stoner

BLUE RIVER PRESS

INDIANAPOLIS, INDIANA

Courthouse Chaos: Famous & Infamous Trial, Mob Violence & Justice

Published by Blue River Press
Indianapolis, Indiana
www.brpressbooks.com

Distributed by Cardinal Publishers Group
A Tom Doherty Company, Inc.
www.cardinalpub.com

LCCN:201957261

ISBN: 978-1-168157-176-8

Book Design: Glen Edelstein
Editors: Dani McCormick

Printed in the United States of America

10 9 8 7 6 5 4 3 2 1 20 21 22 23 24 25 26 27 28 29

Dedicated to the hundreds of federal, state and local government officials I had the privilege to work alongside for nearly two decades. As former US Representative Lee H. Hamilton of Indiana said, "I can assure you, public service is a stimulating, proud and lively enterprise. It is not just a way of life, it is a way to live fully."

CONTENTS

INTRODUCTION

The county courthouse—revered as the center of the community, the citadel for justice—has at other times become the bloody setting for the settling of raw human emotions. In an instant, the prestige and distinction of the courthouse is reduced to a violent battlefield.

Herein are some of the stories of the murder, mayhem and mystery that surrounds America's temples of justice—the county courthouse. Whether the cases involved the spectacle of "famous" or "infamous" defendants on trial, or the ugly realization of lynch-style justice on the courthouse lawn, the stories are an integral part of the history of our communities.

In the most basic sense, the county courthouse is simply a public building built for the administration of justice, and the storage and organization of official records—civil and criminal. But as author Ray McDevitt noted, communities pour into their courthouse some of their highest aspirations—the peaceful resolution of disputes, the protection of individuals against abusive or oppressive power, dutiful punishment of wrongdoers, alongside with vindication for the innocent.[1] But in countless moments of desperation, the courthouse has become a place of chaos.

We look beyond the varied nature of America's county and federal courthouses, some of them ornate monuments to a community's largesse, and others blandly efficient office buildings built for functionality and little else. We look also to the trials and tribulations of the buildings themselves, structures that have survived good days and bad to remain the proud centerpiece of the community.

We segue into a brief recap of the events that threaten to tarnish the beauty and aura of the courthouse before diving into the root causes of what prompted the tragic events. A human drama of some kind unfolds every day in America's courthouses where the corridors are filled with the highest, most powerful members of the community walking alongside some of the most desperate and dangerous citizens to be found.

Some of the backstories will be familiar—failed marriages, business and political rivalries, gang violence, and men and women whose lives are spiraling out of control. And others represent the unresolved and simmering issues of race and privilege played out in deadly, sickening fashion. Few of the cases represent "career criminals," but rather "everyday people" whose lives explode in a *very* public way, and a *very* public place—the county courthouse.

—Andrew E. Stoner
October 2019

TRIALS

The "Trial" of Thrill Killers Leopold & Loeb

COOK COUNTY CRIMINAL COURT BUILDING
July to September, 1924—Chicago, Illinois

The stately Richardson Romanesque Criminal Court Building at 54 West Hubbard Street in Chicago served as a predictable, if not unglamorous setting for what was supposed to be one of the great trials of the twentieth century.

Between the scorching hot months of July to September 1924, famed attorney Clarence Darrow successfully argued to save the lives of two troubled and privileged killers, Nathan Leopold, twenty years old, and Richard Loeb, nineteen.

The "trial," however, became little more than a sentencing hearing as the two accused killers surprised everyone and changed their plea to guilty in an ultimately successful attempt to avoid the death penalty.

"Leopold and Loeb," as they became known as their case gained fame, were two University of Chicago students who abducted and later killed an eleven-year-old boy from their well-heeled Chicago neighborhood. Robert "Bobby" Franks knew his killers and went willingly with them for a car ride on May 21, 1924 and was never seen alive again.

Their plans for the "perfect crime" quickly falling apart, Leopold and Loeb cooperated with police and prosecutors and provided graphic details of their murder of Franks which had started as an attempted kidnapping. In fact, key evidence against the men was a letter demanding $10,000 in ransom for the boy sent to the wealthy Franks family.

By the time the trial approached in July 1924, hundreds of reporters and photographers from across the nation descended on Chicago for what was expected to be a spectacular trial. In the naivety of 1920s America, many struggled to understand how it was possible two well-educated and wealthy young men could be involved in such an ugly affair.

The setting for the expected spectacle was the brick, six-story Cook County Criminal Court Building, opened in 1893 and showing the signs of its age. The courtroom for the trial was the air-conditioning free top floor of the building (which was eventually vacated in 1929 with the completion of the new Criminal Court Building on 26th Street, west of the Loop).[1]

Cook County State's Attorney Robert E. Crowe, elevated to office with the help of Chicago's powerful Republican Mayor, "Big Bill" Thompson, had spent months preparing for a trial to prove the men guilty of what he termed "the direst murder in the history of Chicago."[2] Crowe, only forty-five years old at the time, had something to prove—the lead attorney for the defense would be famed, yet aging lawyer Clarence Darrow (sixty-seven years old in 1924).

On Monday, July 21, 1924, an overflow crowd filled the sidewalks and the traffic lanes of Hubbard Street at the front of the Criminal Court Building.

The crowd grew so large, "emergency police were ordered out to handle the throngs massed before the Criminal Court Building. . . . Several score newspapermen and a dozen attorneys were in court where the case was called, but space reserved for spectators was only partly filled. Police precautions were responsible for this condition," an Associated Press dispatch from Chicago told the nation. "Outside the building, hundreds of curious persons gathered in a compact mass about the entrancc. Three policemen on guard were kept busy pushing the crowd back and clearing a space about the doors so that those who had business within might enter."[3]

Circuit Court Judge John R. Caverly announced strict rules for his courtroom which included no one allowed to be admitted without a signed ticket from him, and no one allowed to stand. The judge did allow news photographers to take still photos, but strictly prohibited flashbulbs and sternly tossed out motion picture cameramen who attempted to enter.

As the day opened, Caverly asked for any motions from the defense, and Darrow pulled a major surprise out of his pocket, announcing his clients wished to change their pleas from "not guilty" to "guilty."

To a rapt courtroom and stunned prosecution team led by Crowe, Darrow told the judge his clients understood the implications of their plea and said they were willing to admit to the facts of the case "substantially as printed in the newspapers." Darrow said his only request would be to seek permission "to offer evidence as to the mental condition of these young men and their degree of responsibility."[4]

State's Attorney Crowe vehemently objected to Darrow's suggestion that mental capacity could be a factor once a guilty plea had been entered. Under Illinois law at the time, mental illness could not be considered as a factor in a crime when the defendant had entered a guilty plea.

Crowe barked, "If there is any question as to the sanity of these boys, the state's attorney demands that a jury of twelve men be selected so that the state can prove beyond all shadow of a doubt that Nathan Leopold and Richard Loeb are sane."[5]

"The state is in a position to show that these boys are not only guilty of the facts which they here admit, but that, beyond any reasonable doubt, they are sane and fully cognizant of the consequences of these acts."[6]

Darrow seemed amused that he had caught prosecutors by surprise with the guilty plea and assured the court, "These boys as they now are, are not fit to mingle in society and we will make no effort to set them free."[7]

As the attorneys fought over the guilty pleas entered, reporters focused on Leopold and Loeb and noted both men appeared to have gained weight while in jail, but also looked "markedly pale."[8]

An Associated Press report shared, "Leopold's eyes, which have been considered unusually bright and searching, were watery," as the guilty plea was entered by Darrow. "He gazed into space without apparently seeing anyone. His aged father, the millionaire President of the Morris Paper Box Company, sat silently in the courtroom, tears trickling down his wrought face."[9]

The AP description continued, "Loeb, somewhat taller and more erect, faced the court with more composure. His eyes did not waver from Judge Caverly as he declared that he understood the consequences of pleading guilty to murder. . . . Loeb's father, Albert H. Loeb, multi-millionaire vice president of Sears Roebuck & Company, was not present. The elder Loeb is seriously ill with heart trouble."[10]

Although the judge said his courtroom would not be reduced to a "side show," Caverly nonetheless had to know the drama he was introducing by requiring that both Leopold and Loeb take the stand and formally enter their guilty pleas, rather than just accept Darrow's motion.

"Is it your understanding that if you plead guilty to murder in this court, the court may sentence you to death or to the penitentiary for the period of your natural life or for a period of not less than fourteen years?" Caverly asked Leopold.[11]

Reporters noted Leopold's lips quivered as he said, "Yes, I understand," the same response Loeb offered moments later.

"With this understanding, do you still wish to plead guilty?" the judge asked both men, and both affirmed they did.[12]

Outside the courtroom, Darrow was frank with the cadre of reporters about his reasoning for the guilty plea—noting that the parents of the two young men "did not want the court to impose the death penalty." He said the families also sought to avoid having them declared insane—"a blot that would taint their families forever."[13]

"When I first heard of the crime, I thought some moron had done it," Darrow said, "and I hoped he would not be caught, for I knew what sort of trial he would get. When I learned that it was these two, I was glad they had been found out, because with their natures, they would be sure to do it again."[14]

Back in court, Caverly granted Darrow's request to present "evidence demonstrating the degree of responsibility and evidence of an irresponsibility" in the defendants. "Having presented this evidence, we shall throw ourselves on the mercy of the court," Darrow said. "The defense fully realize[s] that the defendants should be permanently isolated from society."[15]

Although their guilt was no longer a question to be answered, interest in the trial remained intense. The Associated Press moved a story across the nation detailing the spectacle unfolding in Chicago:

> The tiny courtroom, paneled with light oak, on the sixth floor of the dilapidated Criminal Court building,

> just outside Chicago's Loop, was jammed almost to suffocation. . . . The [courtroom] crowd was slow to grasp the meaning of Darrow's statement [of the boy's guilt] and the judge broke out in a loud voice, declaring, 'This is a courtroom, not a side show.' . . . Morbidly curious throngs stampeded the dimly lighted corridors of the Criminal Court Building fighting for a chance to view the prologue to the trial, one of the most sensational cases in the modern history of crime. Hundreds of people gained admission to the building itself. Other hundreds were lined up along the sidewalk, hoping against hope they could enter. Court was not to open until ten o'clock, but at eight a.m., fully 1,000 people were in line, with thousands more expected. Impetuous men and women refused to wait for elevator service to start and plodded their way up six flights of stairs to gain admission to Judge Caverly's court. They were repulsed at the head of the stairs and forced to wait their turn. . . . The courtroom itself was in readiness. Reserved seats for more than 100 newspaper reporters, special correspondents, and feature writers were roped off. Telegraph instruments, equipped with noiseless sounders, were operating.[16]

Despite the change of plea, Caverly permitted the state to present its own parade of witnesses, most of them not even needed to prove the case, but were called nonetheless. Observers suggested the judge had done so since Crowe and his staff had amassed a witness list of nearly 100 people to testify as they had expected to have to prove guilt amidst the expected "not guilty" plea.

With the challenge of proving guilt off the table, the state brought emotional testimony regardless, including the tearful accounts of the mother and father of Bobby Franks, and the ransom letter the

Franks family had received was also read in court. All background testimony regarding Leopold and Loeb served to impeach them as privileged, poorly adjusted young men.

The homosexual relationship between Leopold and Loeb was suggested at times, but never directly addressed in court. It was also factored into the "alienists" reports that were allowed (though psychological reports prepared in support of their guilt were limited since the men had changed their plea to guilty).

Giggles and exchanged looks crossed the courtroom, however, during testimony that revealed "Dickie" Loeb often referred to Leopold as "Baby" or "Babe" in their intensely personal interactions. Expert testimony also revealed both boys had experienced sexual interaction with adults and other children before and just after puberty.

Psychiatric reports on the two men indicated Leopold viewed Loeb as a "master" or "King" and saw himself as a "slave" in their relationship. Both men engaged sadistic fantasies and showed disrespectful attitudes toward young women they knew.

Friends and college classmates also testified and provided little help in portraying the young men in any positive light—some of them calling them "cuckoo" or "intensely vain" men who thought themselves better than all others.[17]

As the state pressed on in making its case, the normally calm Nathan Leopold lost his composure on the seventeenth day of the proceedings. Believing him to be weeping, the judge granted a motion for a recess.

Back in a holding cell in the courts building, Leopold explained he was not crying: "It amused me to see Mr. Crowe's endeavor to twist isolated facts into a contradiction of terms. I began to laugh. Then I breathed. And my breath, instead of going down my wind-pipe, went down my esophagus. And I choked. I am laughing now to think what a spectacle I must have made of myself in the courtroom."[18]

As the case proceeded, crowds diminished. An AP report indicated, "Rain outdoors and the prospect of less dramatic developments in the hearing . . . combined today to dampen enthusiasm of 'court fans.' Police guards which kept the curious on the sidewalks and the knowledge that only a few could gain admission to Judge Caverly's court contributed to this result. Only a knot of curious stood about the building entrance this morning and they were mostly young men."[19]

The hot and humid summer weather in Chicago was taking its toll. Jacob Franks, the victim's father, seemed particularly overwhelmed by heat in the courtroom as he testified, and reporters noted police officers had sweated through their uniform shirts.

"This early morning is hot," *The Chicago Tribune* told its readers. "It is hot on the pavements about the doleful Criminal Courts Building and hot on the backs of the policemen who stand guard in the street, on curbs, and on the sidewalks."[20]

Only spectators holding a pink-colored pass were admitted. "They form a small lane at the entrance of the building. Those that enter have pink tickets signed by the judge. A pink ticket gives one a sense of the profound and important. The police make you show your pink ticket and you are glad to do it; so many have none."[21]

Between court hearings, reporters continued to gain considerable access to the two defendants in holding cells at the Criminal Court Building. Both men seemed strangely comfortable sitting inside jail cells either reading books or newspaper accounts of their trial, or playing cards, oblivious to the perilous future ahead of them.

The Chicago Tribune ran an article that said the high temperatures in the courtroom were all that seemed to bother the two young men, declaring "otherwise they feel fine."[22] A few days later, reporters again spent time with the men at the jail, noting that though the court proceedings were tiresome at times, they were required to stay at attention. *The Chicago Tribune* reported:

> When the boys returned to their cells at Noon, they sat down to hearty meals their parents sent up. Fried chicken, French-fried potatoes, lettuce, coffee, and cake comprised the meal. After the meal, newspapers. Shortly before two o'clock, they took a refreshing shower. When the prisoners were returned to the 'bullpen' they enjoyed an indoor baseball game.[23]

Loeb commented casually: "It's a relief to get a chance to take life easy. The trial is great stuff, but a little rest is good for the best of us."[24]

Thirty-two days after the opening of the matter (and after a remarkable closing statement from Darrow that lasted twelve hours), Judge Caverly ordered heavy security for the reading of the verdict and said the courtroom should be cleared "of all persons not immediately interested in the proceedings."[25]

As *The Tribune* noted, "While the world outside [the courthouse] is waiting for Judge Caverly's decision, the two slayers spent the day reading and playing athletic games with other prisoners."[26]

The Tribune and WGN Radio warned their readers and listeners to be ready for an "almost simultaneous" reading of the verdict over the air from their studio at the Drake Hotel which was connected by telephone to the courtroom.

"Extraordinary precautions were completed last night to insure the safety of Judge John R. Caverly and to prevent any untoward outbreak in or near the Criminal Court Building," *The Tribune* shared. Newspaper accounts included details that the judge would be transported from his apartment at the Edgewater Beach Hotel by a Chicago Police officer, along with "two 'dead shot' detectives in plain clothes" to protect the judge from any violence.[27]

"The first line of police guards surrounding the courthouse will be encountered at Dearborn and Illinois streets," reporters noted. "A group of mounted policemen will give way to [the auto carrying the judge] as it turns into Austin Avenue and pulls up in front of the building. Approximately a hundred police, mounted and on foot, will be stationed about the building to prevent any demonstration by 'cranks' or others."[28]

Loeb's parents, particularly his mother, were in frail health and made the decision to return to their summer vacation home across Lake Michigan at tony Charlevoix, Michigan. "Far away from the drone of the courtroom where the slayers have been fighting for their lives. . . . On their summer estate . . . the father and mother will sit awaiting the tinkle of a telephone bell which will tell them whether their son shall forfeit his life to a hangman or to the walls of Joliet penitentiary."[29]

Loeb's brother Alan would remain at the courtroom and told reporters his mother had sent a special message to her imperiled son: "Tell Dickie, my boy, that we are praying for him and hoping beyond hope that his life will be spared."[30]

In the end, Judge Caverly's decision was long, but anti-climactic as he sentenced both men to life terms. Reporters seemed almost disappointed there were no hysterics or drama at the close of the trial. Ernest Loeb, Richard's brother, seemed to capture the mood well in explaining how his parents had reacted to the verdict:

> It was neither a blow to them, nor was it a message of great cheer. It was, in a sense, the news of a victory, yet it left them in despair. It was a mite of comfort that Dick was not to be hanged. Still [Dick] is only nineteen and must go to prison for life—and the great hurt of the uselessness of this family tragedy remained.[31]

Initially, Leopold and Loeb had little contact with one another in prison, but officials eventually relented and both men contributed to developing a high school and college-level educational curriculum for fellow prisoners. Both men were cut off financially by their wealthy families—in part for their own good since Loeb's cellmate James E. Day often stole or extorted money from him.

Loeb was murdered a dozen years into his sentence, slashed to death on January 28, 1936 by Day, who attacked Loeb in a prison washroom. Loeb was only thirty years old.

Day later told authorities he had killed Loeb for continued unwanted sexual advances, though other reports indicated Day had routinely "bullied" Loeb for years prior to the deadly encounter.

Leopold would make his first and only trip outside of an Illinois state prison cell after Loeb was murdered. His looks had changed so much the editors of *The Chicago Tribune* felt compelled to print a white arrow on their photo of Leopold so readers could recognize him. The February 19, 1936 photograph showed Leopold entering the Will County Courthouse at Joliet to testify before a grand jury investigating the prison slaying of Loeb.[32]

"Leopold was taken before the Will County grand jury . . . to tell what he knew of the motive behind the razor slaying of Loeb," *The Tribune* reported. Will County State's Attorney Will R. McCabe quickly learned Leopold was unwilling to share any information and was returned to jail. Reporters described Leopold as "morose," and that he attempted to bury his face in the pulled up collar of his overcoat as photographers shot dozens of frames.[33]

Attorneys in the courtroom described Leopold as polite, but anti-social.

As he entered the courthouse, Leopold griped to reporters out of the side of his mouth: "I don't like the idea of having a lot of guys shoot questions at me. I wish I were back in the big house."[34]

Before grand jurors, Leopold refused to detail what he witnessed in Loeb's cell when Day allegedly made an "appointment" to meet Loeb in the men's washroom.[35]

Three decades after the Leopold and Loeb ended, Genevieve Forbes Herrick, a rare female reporter in 1920s Chicago, looked back on her work in writing up every aspect of the trial for readers of the city's largest daily, *The Chicago Tribune*. The old Cook County Criminal Courts Building was "a shabby set" for the show, Herrick said. She said the trial took place in:

> A small courtroom of the old Criminal Courts Building reached by a worn stairway that creaked under its daily load of people hoping to sneak into the trial. Or by a rickety elevator, run by a rickety old man, carrying the privileged who held precious cards of admittance. In that courtroom, the air was sometimes so foul from sweating humanity that when the dirty windows were raised, the aroma from neighboring fish markets was refreshing.[36]

Herrick said Loeb attracted a gaggle of admiring young females who struggled to get a courtroom seat, and called him by the affectionate name "Dickey." She said "their affectionate diminutive is indicative of their foolish frenzy," she said. "Nobody gave Leopold a diminutive—he never even was called Nathan—just Leopold."[37]

Older audience members were interested to hear Clarence Darrow, a colorful character known for his ruffled look. Darrow did tell reporters outside the courtroom, "I don't see what's the matter? I get my suits made by the best tailors [but] of course, I sleep in them."[38]

Leopold and Loeb were not handcuffed during the trial, state's attorneys concerned that doing so could prejudice the proceedings (even though it was heard before a judge, with no jury seated).

Herrick said she watched the two defendants closely:

> For weeks, I sat so near Leopold that my hand could have brushed his sleeve. I could have seen every change of expression on his face, but there was no change. I did see the doodles he made on the pad of paper on which he took notes. I heard his whispered comments and criticisms to his attorneys. We never spoke. He never nodded. He was indifferent, seemed surly. When you sit next to a man on trial for his life, for many weeks, it is difficult for you to want him to get the death penalty. But a reporter, like a doctor or undertaker, must be professionally objective.[39]

The young female reporter said she felt sympathy for the parents of not only the victim, but also of Leopold and Loeb who seemed frozen and shocked by what was happening. While Loeb's father Jacob tried to keep busy, volunteering to do errands for Darrow, he still always looked as if he was about to burst into tears.

Leopold won release from prison in March 1958 after serving just over thirty-three years—he was fifty-three years old. Upon release, he accepted a position with the Brethren Service Commission of the Church of the Brethren, a Protestant pacifist group based in Puerto Rico.[40] Earlier in 1958 he released an autobiography titled, *Life Plus 99 Years* meant to support his requests for parole.

Remaining in Puerto Rico because of the anonymity it gave him, in 1963 Leopold wrote a second book reflecting his interest in ornithology, *Checklist of Birds of Puerto Rico and the Virgin Islands*. He died of a heart attack on August 29, 1971 at the age of sixty-six.

A Planned Spectacle of a Trial

RHEA COUNTY COURTHOUSE

July 6–21, 1925—Dayton, Tennessee

There may have been some who believed the now-legendary "Scopes Monkey Trial" at the Rhea County Courthouse in Dayton, Tennessee was really about the legality of teaching the theory of evolution in public schools.

Most observers, however, quickly recognized the spectacle unfolding in the tiny southern Tennessee town had little to do with justice, and more to do with making a point on either side of the origin of humankind. Evolutionists were eager to challenge Tennessee's new state law that strictly forbid the teaching of evolution in public schools, while creationists were excited for a chance to proclaim the gospel's version of how human life was the literal creation of God.

The debate had been incited by a bill passed by members of the 1924 Tennessee legislature, known as the "Butler Act" named for its author, State Representative John W. Butler, a farmer and devout fundamentalist Christian. The bill was enacted, it seems, without consideration that the bill directly contradicted the officially approved biology textbook for Tennessee high schools.[41]

The Dayton, Tennessee setting for the challenge to the "Butler Act" couldn't be more Americana if it had been scripted by a Hollywood producer. As the Associated Press reported, "The courthouse site is half-concealed by a grove of leafy elm, oak, poplar, and sweet gum trees, which shade the fenced-in, grass-grown square. Just in front of the main entrance of the red-brick structure is a long-handled water pump."[42]

Officially captioned Scopes versus the State of Tennessee, the man at the center of the trial, John T. Scopes, ultimately became an afterthought amidst high-powered celebrity representatives on both sides of the issue. Scopes, a Kentucky native, had come to the small Tennessee town in 1924 to become the football coach at Rhea County High School.

As part of his duties, Scopes filled in teaching in classrooms when the regular instructors were unavailable. One of the classes where he "subbed" was a biology class that officially had a textbook that provided an account of evolutionary theory, although Scopes was never fully clear whether he had actually taught the concept in detail, or briefly mentioned it in class.[43]

If the trial of Scopes on violation of the state's Butler Act was a show, so was the original charge. The American Civil Liberties Union even placed advertisements seeking a Tennessee school teacher willing to assist in challenging the validity of the law.[44] Supporters of evolution recruited high school students to file official "complaints" against Scopes for having taught the theory in class—but only after a group of local evolutionists talked Scopes into agreeing to be tried on the misdemeanor charge (which carried a maximum fine of $100 to $500).[45]

Evolutionists had convinced famed criminal defense attorney Clarence Darrow, an avowed agnostic, to assist in the defense of Scopes. Meanwhile, creationists easily attracted the support of "the Commoner," William Jennings Bryan, a former Presidential candidate and known widely for his devout Christian beliefs.

The leaders of Dayton—regardless of their views on the origin of mankind—seemed more than happy to play along. News reports across the nation highlighted how the town (with a population of just 1,700 in the 1920s) prepared in earnest for the Scopes trial.

"The town of Dayton, nestling in the foothills of the Appalachians, has made extensive preparations to stage the trial and receive the hundreds of visitors the case is expected to attract," an Associated Press dispatch explained. "Dayton has experienced one of those metamorphoses known to . . . other little out-of-the-way places to which fate brings the sudden glare of the spotlight of human interest."[46]

Dayton recruited police officers from Chattanooga and other communities to help direct traffic and keep the peace—reporters noting that the town's one police officer also served as superintendent of the water works and street departments. "Fashionably dressed visitors in smart motor cars drive through the narrow streets [of Dayton], tourists who want to send home a post card from the scene of the Scopes trial," newspaper reports shared.[47]

As a central issue of the trial was whether man had evolved from lower forms of beings, such as apes or monkeys, local merchants played along. "Shop windows are filled with monkey this and monkey that, monkey umbrella handles, neckties with monkey designs, and so on," the AP reported.[48]

In addition to hot dog and soda stands sprouting up along Main Street and on the courthouse lawn[49], one local church rebuffed an effort to lease its fellowship hall to an enterprising Chattanooga man. The man "tried to lease a church tabernacle to convert it into an all-night dance hall and cabaret. But the deacons would not hear of it. They want to serve meals [in the church] at seventy-five cents a head."[50]

Some local expectations were understandably disappointed. Estimates that as many as 5,000 visitors would crowd the town turned out to be more like 500—most of them news reporters. One disappointment was avoided, however, as locals had worried that "damn Yankee" lawyers from the north would attempt to get the case removed from Dayton and transferred to a federal court.[51]

Some outsiders were unimpressed with Dayton—the AP running a photograph of the Rhea County Courthouse describing it as "sad" given that the courtroom lacked the capacity to seat all who were expected to attend.

Locals were taking full advantage—one hotel raising its prices to eight dollars a day (including meals), or five dollars a day without meals. One local group, the Dayton Progressive Club, installed a banner over Main Street advising visitors to check with them about room rates—promising shared rooms for as little as two dollars a day, plus seventy-five cents for meals.[52]

At the courthouse, activity continued to buzz as electricians installed miles of wires to allow *The Chicago Tribune*, via WGN Radio of Chicago, to broadcast the trial live (a first-of-its-kind effort in the US).

"An open-air auditorium—including platform and bench seats—had been built on the north side of the courthouse to accommodate the public in a number of ways," the AP reported. "Those invited to make public addresses, of political, scientific or theoretical nature will be heard. Band concerts will be given at intervals in the court sessions. Amplifiers will relay reports of the court proceedings for the benefit of those unable to get seats inside [the courthouse]."[53]

Reporters also noted that the courthouse clock was more than a little out of order. "At regular intervals, loud ringing tones from the courthouse steeple announce the hour to Dayton folk—and announce it consistently thirty-five minutes ahead of Central Standard Time. . . . The white-faced [courthouse] clock is unprotected by cover of any kind. Sparrows hop and flutter on its rusty hands which wind and rain have beat upon for years."[54]

Understanding the political nature of the proceedings, the "Anti-Evolution League" set up a temporary headquarters inside a store front opposite the courthouse, organized by fire-and-brimstone evangelist T. T. Martin of Blue Mountain, Mississippi. During the trial itself, reporters noted that Martin's fundamentalist zeal could grow so loud that "his voice exhorting the audience [on the courthouse lawn] sometimes penetrated to the courtroom."[55]

"Here and there in the throng that milled about the Rhea County Courthouse, one could single out the beaming features of William Jennings Bryan, the stooped figure of Clarence Darrow, or catch a glimpse of the young broad-shouldered, serious-minded defendant [Scopes], as well-wishers pushed forward to shake his hand," a Missouri reporter shared with his readers.[56]

With more than a little irony, Judge John T. Raulston gaveled the trial to order just after 9 a.m. on Friday, July 10, by first calling on a local pastor to offer an invocation.

"The Tennessee pastor, in a voice that boomed through the

courtroom, called on God to direct the course of the trial and give wisdom to the judge and jury," the AP reported. "'Every good and perfect gift cometh down from the Holy Father of life. Thou art the source of our inspiration and power,' [the pastor said]. 'We are incapable of performing pure thoughts and religious deeds without thine aide. We beseech thee, oh Father, to give this court a sufficient measure of the divine spirit as will enable it to administer justice with wisdom to all and that God's standard of justice and holiness will be upheld."[57]

Judge Raulston then signaled Sheriff R. B. Harris to deliver an unnamed four-year-old boy who was perched on the judge's bench. The little boy "drew slips from a hat and the sheriff summoned the men so picked from the first panel waiting in the room. When thirteen men were drawn. . . . [and] the new jury assembled, Judge Raulston then read the first chapter of Genesis from a battered old Bible he brought to the courtroom."[58]

A bank of news reporters and teletype operators lined the courtroom, in addition to the microphones installed to allow the live radio broadcast of the proceedings. Among the packed room of spectators were a former justice of the Mississippi Supreme Court and a sitting federal judge from Louisiana. Former Tennessee Governor and Congressman Benton McMillin also drew a lot of attention as he shook hands at the courthouse with dozens of locals.[59]

Judge Raulston seemed to allow a rather loose arrangement, not objecting to a burst of applause that broke out among the courtroom observers upon the entrance of Bryan. *The Chicago Tribune* assessed matters this way: "This will be a shirt sleeve, collarless trial. Everything goes but smoking in the courtroom" noting the unforgiving temperatures outside the courthouse hovering near 100 degrees.[60] Eventually the judge allowed additional fans to be placed in the courtroom in an attempt to provide relief, but most continued to suffer.[61]

Raulston had overseen a brief upgrade of his courtroom before the throng of out-of-towners arrived. "The courtroom has been rebuilt, repapered, cleansed of its ancient tobacco juice and divested of its rusty stoves and presents a neat and attractive appearance" *The Chicago Tribune* reported.[62]

Bryan had readily agreed to participate in the trial—assisting other lawyers officially in charge of convicting Scopes. "The hand which writes the pay check should rule the schools," Bryan had told several audiences. "The teachers are employees of the taxpayers and should no more be allowed to teach what they personally wish than a clerk should be allowed to dictate the policy of a bank. The greatest menace we have to face today is the substitution of education for religion."[63]

Darrow and the attorneys assembled by the ACLU were present to raise "the question whether the Tennessee legislature has the power to prevent the young minds of Tennessee from knowing what has been thought and said by the world's greatest scientists, [and] preventing them from forming their own judgment in regard to questions of life and science."[64]

Most news accounts of the trial focused little on the actual testimony as the proceedings devolved into a showdown between Darrow and Bryan.

Further stealing attention away from the matter at hand was an unusual declaration by Judge Raulston that the crowd gathered for the case was so large it posed a threat to the structural integrity of the courthouse.[65]

"An unmanageable crowd so filled the courtroom Monday afternoon that Judge Raulston became alarmed and ordered all outdoors," *The Indianapolis News* reported. "The Rhea County Courthouse is an old building and the floor is said to be none too strong. When the crowd reached the point that almost as many persons were standing as were seated [in the courtroom], a report was made to the court that plastering was falling from the ceiling [in the room] below."[66]

Raulston, concerned by reports that the floor of the courthouse might "collapse at any moment," ordered the proceedings to adjourn to the bandstand constructed on the courthouse lawn by anti-evolutionists.

"A memorable scene was enacted yesterday afternoon beneath the great maples that canopy the yard of the Rhea County Courthouse," wrote *St. Louis Post-Dispatch* correspondent Paul Y. Anderson (an eventual Pulitzer Prize winner). "On a crude platform where was convened the trial of John T. Scopes, Clarence Darrow placed William Jennings Bryan on the witness stand, and what followed was an event in the intellectual history of the world. It was magnificent and tragic, stirring and pathetic, and above all, it was pervaded by the atmosphere of grandeur which befitted a death grapple between two great ideas."[67]

Judge Raulston, who had refused to allow a large portion of testimony from Bible scholars, did allow the state to call Bryan as a Biblical expert to be cross-examined under the blazing Tennessee sun by Darrow.

Anderson described the two great lions as "old, magnetic and passionate men" who championed their ideas for and against the theory of evolution "remorselessly." It was an uneven match, however, even though Darrow, at 68 years of age, was three years older than Bryan. As Anderson wrote "Let there be no doubt about it, Bryan was broken if ever a man was broken. Darrow never spared him. It was masterful, but it was pitiful."[68]

Anderson added sadly, "It was profoundly moving to see this wonderful man [Bryan], for after all he was wonderful, this man whose silver voice and majestic mien had stirred millions to see him humbled and humiliated before the vast crowd which had come to adore him, was sheer tragedy, nothing else."[69]

The testimony of Bryan was predictable—that the Bible was the unquestioned and literal word of God—including the Biblical story of creation of all men emanating from Adam and Eve in the Garden of Eden. Darrow, equally expected, raised pointed questions about each of Bryan's beliefs.

As spectacular as the exchange between Bryan and Darrow was, it was all conducted outside of the company of the jury. The judge refused to allow them to hear the testimony but interestingly allowed it outside of their presence "for the record" and "to show the higher courts what the defense could have presented had they been allowed to introduce expert witnesses on the Bible and evolution."[70]

Bryan said to applause, "I am here to defend religion. I am willing to answer every question."[71] Bryan accused Darrow and those who refused ideas of Godly creation of mankind as trying to insult creationists as "bigots" and "intolerant ignoramuses." Darrow responded in kind that Bryan "insults every scientist and every man of learning in the world."[72]

The interaction between the two men escaped the gentlemanly nature of things prior to that day, with Bryan growing angry at repeated questions about the validity of the Bible tale of Jonah escaping the stomach of a giant whale. Bryan declared, "[I] don't know whether it was a big fish or not, but I know that God could make a man or a whale do anything he wanted. I want the world to know that I will not let an atheist and agnostic question me at any time about the Bible!"[73]

Darrow responded with an equally angry retort to Bryan: "No one else believes in your fool ideas!"[74]

With that the several thousand spectators gathered around the courthouse "became acrimonious" and Judge Raulston had had enough—after two hours of sparring between the men—and adjourned the proceedings.

At the conclusion of eight days of testimony in as raucous a setting as ever recorded in a court anywhere, the jury took just nine minutes to find Scopes guilty. The judge set his fine at $100. Both the sentence and the fine were later overturned on appeal.

Both Darrow and Bryan had hoped to use the occasion of the Scopes trial to further their public speaking engagements and prominence in American life. Bryan was unable to undertake many speaking engagements, however, as he died unexpectedly at his home on July 26, 1925, just five days after the close of the Scopes trial. He was sixty-five years old.

Darrow continued to practice as a lawyer for another decade, though his prominence continued to decline along with his health. He died in Chicago on March 13, 1938 at the age of eighty.

Bringing Down "The Law" In Indiana

HAMILTON COUNTY COURTHOUSE

October-November 1925—Noblesville, Indiana

David Curtis Stephenson, better known as "D.C. Stephenson," staged a meteoric rise and an equally spectacular demise during a short but amazing period of the 1920s when the Ku Klux Klan took its racist power to its zenith in Indiana.

Stephenson, who once declared that, "I am the law in Indiana!" met his final downfall in two of the stateliest courthouses in the state, first during a spectacular trial in 1925 at the Hamilton County Courthouse in Noblesville, Indiana.

Two years later, Stephenson made good on his threats to expose state and local officials who had benefitted from the growing political largesse the KKK brought in the 1920s during a surprise hearing at the Marion County Courthouse in Indianapolis.

Stephenson's success was for real—between 1922 and 1923—the Klan added more than 2,000 paid members every week in each of Indiana's ninety-two counties.[75] Named "Grand Dragon" of the Indiana Klan before a crowd estimated at 100,000 on July 4, 1923 at Kokomo, Indiana, Stephenson had built the Indiana Klan to include as many as 300,000 members statewide—in some counties, up to one-third of the male population were among the Klan faithful.

"D.C. Stephenson was preoccupied with the cultivation of power and money, both of which he seemed to have in abundance, at least for a short time," historian Leonard J. Moore wrote. "As a result of his association with the Klan between 1922 and 1924, he probably accumulated more than one million dollars which he used to support a lifestyle that was grossly at odds with the traditional values for which the Klan claimed to stand."[76]

That conflict of values played out in the worst way in 1925 and ultimately cost the life of Madge Oberholtzer, a twenty-nine-year-old unmarried Indianapolis woman. As Moore wrote, "The horrible details of Oberholtzer's assault and death, combined with Stephenson's arrogant, unremorseful statements to the press during his trial [for her death], repelled citizens throughout Indiana and badly damaged the Klan's reputation."[77]

Oberholtzer was employed at the time of her death as a little noticed clerk in the Statehouse offices of the State Superintendent of Public Instruction. She still lived with her parents in a well-appointed Indianapolis suburb; one of their prominent neighbors was D. C. Stephenson. She was well liked and at the time of her death was manager of the Young People's Reading Circle of Indiana.

On the evening of March 15, 1925, when Oberholtzer returned home, her mother relayed to her that Stephenson's secretary had called and wanted her to stop over at his home for information related to her work at the Statehouse. Oberholtzer complied, but no ordinary meeting transpired.

During Stephenson's trial, testimony was offered that said Oberholtzer was either drugged or given spiked alcoholic drinks to make her compliant to Stephenson's planned sexual advances. Swooped up against her will, Oberholtzer, Stephenson and one of his minions arrived at Union Station in Indianapolis and boarded a northbound train for Hammond, Indiana (near Chicago). Once aboard the Pullman car train, Oberholtzer was repeatedly raped while the train rumbled through the dark night of northwest Indiana. Arriving in Hammond, Stephenson checked his party into a hotel under a fake name, pretending the dazed Oberholtzer was his wife. In the hours that followed, an additional violent and sadistic rape occurred where Oberholtzer suffered multiple wounds, including severe bite wounds to her body—including her breasts.

In a deathbed statement given many days later, Oberholtzer told of first trying to kill Stephenson, or herself, with his revolver, but then settled on purchasing bichloride mercury from a Hammond drug store in order to end her suffering.

Oberholtzer had planned to take 18 bichloride of mercury tablets, but became ill after ingesting just six. Once Stephenson learned of what she had done, he forced Oberholtzer to drink a bottle of milk in a vain attempt to counteract the mercury. She later told her family that Stephenson refused to take her to a local hospital unless she agreed to lie and say she was Stephenson's wife so no questions would be asked about the hotel liaison.

Deathly ill and with no medical attention, Stephenson instead rented a car and began a lengthy 165-mile drive from

Hammond to Indianapolis. Once at Stephenson's home, Oberholtzer still received no aid and was instead housed overnight in a car garage behind Stephenson's home - while just four blocks away her parents were frantically talking to police about her unknown whereabouts.

The next day, March 17, 1925, one of Stephenson's cronies took Oberholtzer's dying body to her family home, placed her on a bed and said she had been in a traffic accident.

"The girl lingered between life and death at her home while every effort to save her life was made by a family physician," reported *The Indianapolis Star*. The effort was "without avail, and she died at 10:05 the morning of April 14, 1925."[78]

Her death was initially attributed to self-administered mercury poisoning, but state officials later introduced medical testimony that indicated, "She died as much from the results of her alleged mistreatment as from the poison she took afterward."[79]

An Indiana University doctor who assisted in treating Oberholtzer in her dying days, and examined her body after her death, "declared that infection from one of the [bite] lacerations on the [left breast of] girl's body had developed into blood poisoning which spread to her lungs and kidneys."[80]

Stephenson and his two co-conspirators were already under arrest for the abduction and sexual assault charges on the day Oberholtzer died, and so more serious charges were added. Curiously, an arson fire gutted Stephenson's palatial home on the same day Oberholtzer expired—likely to destroy any remaining evidence against the men.

As the trial for Stephenson approached, attorneys mowed through more than 230 Indiana men before settling on the final jury panel consisting of ten farmers, a gas station manager, and a truck driver. So prominent were the jurors that they posed for reporters, as a group, for a formal photograph on the steps of the Hamilton County Courthouse.[81]

"Women were precluded from service [on the jury] because of [a] lack of accommodations in the Hamilton County Courthouse jury room," *The Indianapolis Star* explained. "No women ever have been called on a jury venire in the county."[82]

At trial, defense attorney Eph Inman attempted to convince jurors that Oberholtzer had died as a result of a suicide, not a murder or any act on the part of Stephenson or others. They also called witnesses, most of them trusted Klan allies of Stephenson, who offered testimony that questioned Oberholtzer's personal morals regarding drinking alcohol and engaging in sex with men to whom she was not married. They also openly suggested Oberholtzer had "romantic intentions" regarding Stephenson that he had rebuffed previously.

The state was having none of it, prosecutors focusing on witnesses who testified to her virtue, and to subsequent findings that the infection resulting from the severe bite wound inflicted by Stephenson on Oberholtzer's breast was the real cause of death.

Prosecutor Ralph K. Kane did, however, criticize the investigation undertaken by Marion County Coroner Paul F. Robinson for a lack of "any sense of decency." If the coroner were a decent man, Kane said, "He would not have allowed a bunch of newspaper men in an autopsy where the nude body of Madge Oberholtzer was lying on a table. Doctors had a right to be there, but the newspapermen didn't. They couldn't protect that girl even in death."[83]

Perhaps most damning to Stephenson and crew was the "deathbed statement" Oberholtzer reportedly gave to her doctor, who was permitted by the judge to relay the contents of the statement to the jury.

Deputy Prosecutor Charles C. Cox seemed to understand

the importance of the move to allow the statement, declaring to the jurors, "The principal witness for the state will be Madge Oberholtzer, the dead victim of the foulest murder in the history of Indiana. Madge Oberholtzer, standing by the very edge of her grave, will tell you as far as possible under the circumstances the story of her being drugged, kidnapped, assaulted and ravished."[84]

Cox said, "Her story will tell you how she was forced by the loss of all which women hold most dear to take the deadly poison which contributed to her untimely and cruel death."[85]

Prosecutors sought to defame Stephenson beyond what the criminal charges may have already done—Prosecutor Cox described Stephenson as having "a double personality" with "one side of him able to show a magnetic, cultured leader of men. The other side showing him a drunkard, a persistent seducer and destroyer of women's chastity."[86] Cox noted Stephenson sometimes hosted some of the city and state's most powerful Republican leaders and on other occasions hosting "lascivious drinking debauches" where "virgin girls and good women were lured to be entrapped and debauched."[87]

"More than one thousand persons jammed into the little Circuit Court room here to hear the final arguments," reporters offered in an incredible over-statement on the size of the crowd. "Automobiles were parked about the public square [in Noblesville] two and three deep, and [the Sheriff] was busy all day handling, in an efficient manner, the large crowd which stuffed the room."[88]

Among the most compelling witnesses called was Mrs. Matilda Oberholtzer, Madge's grieving mother. In a breathless account, *The Muncie Evening-Star* reported, "In a voice so low it could hardly be heard . . . Mrs. Oberholtzer told of jagged wounds on her daughter's body and deep bruises on her face. The creaking of a chair was the only sound breaking the stillness of the courtroom as she related her daughter's condition."[89]

While defense attorneys avoided any cross-examination of the mother's testimony, they did attempt to introduce evidence that would have called Madge Oberholtzer's "purity" into question. The judge refused to allow such information to be entered, saying the woman's past was immaterial to the charges at hand.

The Muncie Star-Press was equally dramatic in its coverage of the conclusion of the trial: "Women fainted and men fought to get into the courtroom to hear the [final] arguments" where "attorneys threw oral mud at one another, shook their fists in each other's faces, and charged perjury on the part of witnesses."[90]

The trial "was a spectacle that attracted the countryside. So anxious were the spectators to see it, they left their automobiles in the middle of the streets of the town square. Once inside the courthouse, they consumed every inch of space, draping themselves over the judge's desk and mixing with the defendants and attorneys."[91]

Acknowledging the national prominence the trial had generated, prosecutors told jurors that Oberholtzer's death was clearly murder, not a suicide. "On you are the eyes on the state of Indiana—nay, the whole country—for the people want to know whether it is possible for one man or set of men to perpetuate a crime like this and escape the punishment he deserves."[92]

Reporters noted that Stephenson and his co-defendants appeared "unmoved" throughout the blistering closing description of them as "monsters," and the only noteworthy moment was when a four-year-old boy (the son of a reporter covering the trial) wandered away from his father and "sauntered out in front of the jury."[93]

"The boy casually walked over to the defense table, ducked under it and came up in front of Stephenson," the Associated Press reported. "Stephenson took the youngster over to the press table where his dad was working."[94]

After just five hours and thirty-five minutes of deliberations, the jury found Stephenson guilty of second-degree murder, while acquitting co-defendants Earl Gentry and Earl Klinek. Jury deliberations took longer than most expected, and when the verdict came, few spectators were present. Spectators had packed the courtroom throughout the proceedings, however. "Several hundred of the audience ate lunch in the courtroom, refusing to leave while the jury was out, confidently expecting a verdict within a short time," it was reported.[95] The Noblesville post of the Women's Relief Corps used the occasion of the trial to make some money, selling box lunches inside the courthouse corridors.[96]

As usual, Stephenson was not without comment. As reporters shouted questions to him on the courthouse steps, Stephenson declared, "Surrender, hell! We've only begun to fight!"[97]

Noting that he had been the subject of "pernicious hate" beyond which his co-defendants had had to endure, he said, "Everyone knows the circumstances and the atmosphere which surrounded the jury during the entire trial."[98]

Stephenson explained to reporters, "This has not been a lawsuit, but has been an expression of envy, jealousy and malice interwoven with a campaign of propaganda which was pursued with feverish intensity and was designed for no other purpose except to wield an unsavory influence upon the public mind."[99]

"The last chapter has not been written," Stephenson vowed.[100]

As expected, at his sentencing hearing Stephenson had

more to say when the judge asked him if he wished to make a statement. "I have this to say," Stephenson said. "I am not guilty of this charge of murder or any lesser charge of homicide. It has always been my understanding that no man could be deprived of his liberty without due process of law."[101]

Stephenson seemed most bothered by the behavior of the spectators at the trial, noting that some of them "applauded the things said against me and hissed the pleas in my behalf. In this situation, the jury had no way of arriving calmly and impartially at a verdict."[102]

"In the atmosphere that surrounded the entire procedure, a fair and impartial trial was impossible," Stephenson said. "Carefully shielded but powerful influences which converted money into malicious stories and evil propaganda had done their work by influencing a certain element of people."[103]

Defiant to the end, Stephenson vowed, "I want to reiterate that I do not intend to be a sacrificial lamb that will be offered up as a political scapegoat for the whole state of Indiana."[104]

While the judge apologized that any hissing may have occurred (saying his hearing was not good, and he may have missed it), he nonetheless sentenced the once powerful Stephenson to life in prison on November 19, 1925. As the sentence was read, Stephenson "sat calmly in a chair and chewed an unlighted cigar as the judge delivered the sentence."[105]

Following sentencing, Stephenson was transferred to the Indiana State Prison at Michigan City where he continued to file complaints about unfair treatment and inhumane conditions. His legal appeals languished with increasingly diminished chance of success.

Having vowed to not remain in jail, but rebuked in his efforts to win a pardon or other support from Indiana Governor Edward L. Jackson or other state and local officials he had helped elect, Stephenson finally made good on is pledge to "spill the beans."

As *The Indianapolis Star* put it, "D. C. Stephenson, stormy petrel of Indiana politics whose accusations of corruption and graft broadcast from a lifer's cell in the state prison have kept Hoosier officialdom in turmoil, will be brought before the Marion County grand jury to prove his charges."[106]

On July 30, 1927, just two years into his sentence, Stephenson made a dramatic and surprise appearance at the Marion County Courthouse in Indianapolis on a quiet Saturday afternoon. Although it was widely reported he likely would appear before a grand jury investigating graft and corruption among various public officials, his actual arrival failed to produce the crowds his original trial drew.

"After more than five hours of questioning [by the grand jury], Stephenson was hurried away from the courthouse and started on the return trip to Michigan City, in a somewhat dramatic fashion," *The Indianapolis News* reported.[107]

A prison car awaited Stephenson as he left the courthouse "between two guards, led down the stairs and out to the car. As he passed through the corridor of the building, he waved at some acquaintances. He tried to shield his face as a flashlight picture was taken, and his hand trembled."[108]

Although shielded from public view, prosecutors confirmed Stephenson walked jurors through about 7,000 pages of papers contained in five "black boxes" where he kept signed pledges and other records showing bribes and payoffs made to local officials. Stephenson had finally agreed to surrender the boxes from their rural Indiana hiding place after it became clear the powerful men he once called friends were not going to help get him out of jail.

Stephenson's attorney said he had vowed "to go through with what I have started. I purchased the Marion County and [Indiana] state officials in this investigation on an open market. I paid an excessive price for them. Afterward, they railroaded me to prison and convicted me of a crime of which I am not guilty."[109]

Eventually, Stephenson got the final word as Indianapolis Mayor John Duval was forced from office in October 1927 amidst evidence he had taken bribes from the Klan leader to ensure favorable city appointments and contracts.

Governor Jackson stood trial for bribery later in 1927, but was acquitted when it was determined any alleged bribe from Stephenson had been paid outside the statute of limitations in the law. Jackson was ruined, however, and never returned to public life.

Stephenson was finally released from prison in 1950 after having served nearly twenty-five years. He was briefly returned to prison the next year after being cited for a parole violation, but was released again on parole in 1956. Arrested in 1961 in Tennessee on charges of sexually molesting a young woman, the charges were eventually dropped. Stephenson died in obscurity in 1966 at the age of seventy-four.

The Trials of Dr. Sam Sheppard

CUYAHOGA COUNTY CRIMINAL COURTS BUILDING
October–December 1954 and
October–November 1966—Cleveland, Ohio

Handsome Dr. Sam Sheppard went on trial for the brutal murder of his pregnant wife in October 1954 in "a show that would pack Yankee Stadium, but opened in the virtual privacy of a tiny courtroom in the grimy gray pile which is the [Cuyahoga County] Criminal Courts Building."[110]

Sam Sheppard, thirty-years-old on Independence Day 1954, was charged with killing his thirty-one-year-old wife, Marilyn, who was four months pregnant with the couple's second child at the time of her death.

Sam and the former Marilyn Reese met while both were still youngsters, just thirteen years old. They had started a relationship by the time they were students at Cleveland Heights High School and their relationship continued through college and the couple married in 1945. Their son, Sam, Jr. was born in 1947, whom they quickly nicknamed "Chip."

Two years later Sam completed his osteopathic studies and joined his father and two brothers as a doctor at the Bay View Osteopathic Hospital just outside Cleveland. The young couple bought a modest home in Bay Village, described by reporters as "a comfortable suburb seven miles west of Cleveland. [Their] two story, clapboard house fronted on Lake Erie, and there they entertained their friends at beach parties. The Sheppard's were active in the social activities of their suburban community. They belonged to a nearby yacht club. They were both athletically inclined, and only a week before her death Marilyn practiced her water-skiing behind the boat piloted by her husband."[111]

The murder of Marilyn Sheppard inside the upstairs bedroom of her home at 28924 Lake Road in Bay View, Ohio, drew national attention almost from the start. At 5:40 a.m. on July 4, 1954, Sam Sheppard didn't call police, but instead called his next-door neighbor, Bay View Mayor J. Spencer Houk saying, "Get over here quick! I think they've killed Marilyn!"[112]

From the beginning, Sam Sheppard said an intruder had committed the crime.

Also from the beginning, police investigators cast doubt on Sam's story—calling his description of events "vague".

Deputy Cuyahoga County Sheriff Carl Rossbach told reporters that Sam Sheppard said Marilyn's assailant was taller than himself, about six feet, of medium or average weight, wearing a white shirt, and had bushy hair. "That's all he could tell me," Rossbach said. As *The Akron Beacon-Journal* reported, "Police considered the description so vague that no pickup order based on it was put out."[113]

The rest of Sam's story was that as he slept on a davenport in a downstairs living room, he awoke in the early morning hours of July 4 to hear his wife's screams and moans from an upstairs bedroom. Fearing her screams a complication of her pregnancy, Sam said he went upstairs to check on her welfare and found her beaten and lifeless on her twin bed in the couple's bedroom. Asleep in an adjoining room was the couple's seven-year-old son, Chip.

At that moment, Sam Sheppard claimed he was struck from behind and knocked unconscious. He asserted he awakened a short time later and attempted to give chase to the "bushy-haired suspect" who fled out the back of the home down a long flight of stairs to the family's private beach on Lake Erie.

From the start, police found no evidence of a break-in (although Sam Sheppard said it was their practice to keep their doors unlocked when he was at home), and nothing of any significance stolen. It was never clear whether Marilyn had been sexually assaulted—among the many mistakes investigators made was forgoing a physical examination of her body to make such a determination.

Rossbach made sure to tell reporters that the initial interviews police tried to conduct with Sam Sheppard were quickly halted by prominent Cleveland attorney William Corrigan, hired by the Sheppard family in the hours following Marilyn's murder.

Cuyahoga County Corner Samuel R. Gerber also participated in casting doubt on Sam's story. Gerber readily told reporters, "The theory that Mrs. Sheppard may have been murdered by a drug addict seeking narcotics from her husband's medical supplies had been discarded. Morphine sulphate had been found in the doctor's bag, the coroner said, and other sedative drugs had been found in the home" untouched by an intruder.[114]

Gerber would later rule that Marilyn had died of massive head wounds—as many as thirty-five separate blows—from a blunt object.

Sam Sheppard left the hospital on July 7, 1954, three days after the murder, to attend Marilyn's funeral. The next day the Sheppard family offered a $10,000 reward for information in the case. Also on July 8, Sam submitted to police questioning with his attorney present.

The size of the case quickly outgrew the capabilities of the Bay Village Police Department—a city of just 6,917 residents in 1954—and the Cleveland Police Department and the Cuyahoga County Sheriff's Department took over the case.

By July 17, Sam Sheppard was being characterized in media reports as "the number one suspect" in the case, and on July 22, Gerber conducted a surreal coroner's inquest that drew such a large audience, it was conducted in a Cleveland-area school gymnasium.

Sheppard was arrested on July 30, 1954 while he stayed at his parent's home, and *before* an official charge was entered. It wasn't until August 17, however, that an official indictment was rendered by the Cuyahoga County grand jury—causing Sam Sheppard to be arrested again just one day after he had posted a $50,000 bond.

Sheppard, his father Dr. Richard A. Sheppard, and his brothers Richard N. and Steven Sheppard (both also osteopathic doctors like their father) clearly "over managed" Sam's response to the charges. While his brothers diagnosed that Sam had broken his neck during the struggle inside his home on the night Marilyn died, no police physician ever verified that conclusion.

National newspaper columnist Dorothy Kilgallen noted, "Dr. Sheppard's behavior after the crime did more to prejudice him in the minds of those who jump to unreasonable conclusions than any genuine evidence so far known. . . . The attitude of [Sam Sheppard, his father and his brothers] may have been merely professional, but it appeared to be high-handed and evasive."[115]

While he awaited trial, reporters learned that Sheppard "spent much of his time in jail reading hot-rod magazines. A husky former high school athlete, he also whiled away some time playing handball on a prison court."[116]

As the trial opened, locals hoping for a seat in the courtroom were immediately disappointed. As author James Neff described:

> The first morning [of the trial], about fifteen hundred people gathered outside the courthouse at East Twenty-First Street and Payne Avenue, thirty photographers and television cameramen clustered around the [courthouse] entrance of the Sheppard family, the lawyers, police, and anyone connected to the case who managed to push through the crowd and climb sixteen steps to the entrance of the four-story stone building. . . . As a sheriff's deputy brought Dr. Sam [Sheppard] from the jail down the hallway, some teenage girls in the crush spotted him and squealed, 'Oooh, isn't he handsome.'[117]

Scripps-Howard reporter Andrew Tully assessed that:

> an appetite whetted by months of sensational publicity, Cleveland [residents] would pay scalpers prices to see this world series of trials. But once the sixty-odd newsmen from all over the country were accommodated, there was room only for a few stray, and influential, politicians in the square, cheerless courtroom. So the general public will have to get second-hand the story

> of the events in the early morning hours of the Fourth of July that left thirty-one-year-old Marilyn Sheppard a battered, blood-drenched corpse—her life crushed out by blows that, in the words of the coroner, 'splintered her skill and pulpified her brain.'[118]

Despite repeated attempts by Sam's attorneys to delay or move the trial from the Cuyahoga County Criminal Courts building in Cleveland, seventy-year-old judge Edward Blythin rejected all such attempts. Amidst a courthouse swarming with reporters and photographers, including a rare live camera set up for NBC News outside the courthouse, Blythin even allowed photographers to enter the courtroom and shoot whatever pictures they wanted during court recesses.

Judge Blythin declared, "We must make an inquiry [of the potential jurors] themselves" about whether the intense publicity had affected the ability to get a jury. "If we don't try this method, we will show a lack of faith in the jury system—it is one of the shining lights of our democratic process. I believe on the basis of my experience we can get a fair and impartial jury. We will not continue with the trial in this county if it appears the defendant cannot get a fair trial."[119]

The two "star witnesses" of the trial were predictable—Sam Sheppard trying to tell his version of events in his own words, and the words of a discovered "other woman."

Susan Harris, a laboratory technician who had once worked at the Bay View Hospital with Sheppard, lived in Los Angeles at the time of the Sheppard trial. Investigators had quickly uncovered Harris, despite Sheppard's initial denials that he had engaged an extra-marital affair with her. Harris, interestingly, had been more forthright about her sexual relationship with Sheppard.

Harris was first to testify during a jam-packed hearing on

December 1, 1954. News reports made a great many mentions about her physical appearance in court—an Associated Press report describing her as "a pert, freckled twenty-four-year-old" and "slim, auburn-haired and attractive."[120]

Other reports emphasized her clothing, noting "she wore a plain black wool dress with a high neck and a small white fur collar. She walked into the courtroom with her hands folded in front of her. . . . She had arrived at the court an hour before the trial started and was shielded from newsmen and photographers."[121]

Harris told jurors she and Sheppard had been lovers since August 1953, first meeting each other at a laboratory where Harris worked doing laboratory research for Sheppard's hospital. Their sexual liaisons first started in Sheppard's car parked in downtown Cleveland, but also in an apartment above the Fairview Clinic where Harris worked.

Harris said Sheppard wrote a series of love letters to her, and met up with her in Los Angeles and San Diego during a week-long California visit in November 1953. During that visit, she said, Sheppard bought her a ring, a wristwatch and expressed his love for her.

"Testifying in a low, often semi-audible voice, and looking straight ahead, the attractive witness replied 'yes' to a question as to whether Sheppard 'expressed love for you on other occasions,'" the Associated Press reported. Sheppard had talked to her about wanting to get a divorce during his California visit.[122]

"He told me he loved his wife, very much," Harris testified, "but not so much as a wife. He was thinking of a divorce. He wasn't sure if his father would approve."[123]

Courtroom observers watched Sam Sheppard closely during Harris's testimony—noting that he bit his lip at times, made notes on a tablet, or clasped his hands in front of his chest.

"Her eyes straight ahead and away from the defendant, the pretty witness told of going with him on a date to the home of Dr. and Mrs. Arthur Miller, a Los Angeles osteopath and friend of Sheppard."[124]

Harris described having dinner with the Miller's, after which the men played poker. She admitted that although she did not have an overnight bag and that the Miller's knew that Sam Sheppard was married (his wife visiting other family friends in San Francisco at the time), she spent the night with Sam in a guest room in the Miller residence.

"Miss Harris flushed faintly and hesitated slightly before she gave testimony about sharing a bed with Dr. Sheppard," the AP reported.[125]

Details of an extra-marital affair were likely having their effect on a provincial 1950s Ohio jury, even if it was a large city such as Cleveland. It was unclear, however, whether the scorn for such affairs rested more on Sheppard than on Harris.

Other damaging testimony came from one of Marilyn Sheppard's friends, Thomas Weigle, twenty-six years old, who said he witnessed Sam Sheppard being abusive with his son on one occasion. "It was the first time in the nearly seven-week-old trial that any witness has testified the defendant mistreated his wife or their son," reporters noted.[126]

"My wife went into the kitchen with Marilyn," Weigle testified. "We were watching television, a cowboy and Indian picture. Chip was playing the part of an Indian. He was running around the room. I happened to see Sam's left arm over the arm of the chair. Chip playfully slapped him. Sam grabbed him, and pulled him up over his legs and gave him what I thought was an unmerciful beating. . . . Sam became in a rage. He was red in the face. He landed a number of blows."[127]

Finally on December 10, Sheppard himself took the stand. "A heavy hush filled the small courtroom today as Dr. Samuel Sheppard told how he regained consciousness on the floor outside his wife's bedroom on the morning of July 4, then looked inside to see her beaten and bloody," the Associated Press related.[128]

Sheppard's attorney encouraged the young doctor to tell the events in his own words, but it was perhaps his *choice* of words that was somewhat vexing. Sheppard had an almost third-person manner in which he described what he said happened.

"I realized I had been hurt and as I came to some sort of consciousness I looked at my wife," Sheppard explained in a halting voice, almost like telling the story of someone else's experience. "I was immediately fearful for Chip. I went into Chip's room and in some way observed that he was all right. I don't know how I did it."[129]

It was then, Sheppard said, that he heard noise coming from downstairs. "I can't explain my emotions, but I was stimulated to chase or hit whatever was responsible for what had happened," he said oddly.[130]

Instead of just saying he saw the "bushy haired" suspect in his house—he kept using the word "visualizing"—as if he had created or envisioned the scene.

Downstairs, "I visualized a form," he said.

"I was very confused—punchy in the language we use as slang. I was stimulated or drawn to try to chase this person, which I did. . . . It was at this time I had the feeling I could visualize a silhouette that was discernable."[131]

Offering his dramatic version of events where he had chased the suspect down the beach stairs to the waterfront, he said, "I felt I grasped on an immovable object of some kind. There I felt a choking sensation or a twisting sensation. That's all I can remember until I came to in the water."[132]

Just as he had with responding officers on the morning of the murder, Sheppard offered an entirely vague description of the attacker in his home. "I felt it was a relatively large form in dark clothing," he said. "There was evidence of a good-sized head with a bushy appearance on top of his head."

Under questioning by his own attorney and Prosecutor John J. Mahon, Sheppard denied he had ever discussed getting a divorce with anyone, that he had ever "beaten" his son in anger, and denied he had discussed how to fake a head injury (consistent with the one he allegedly suffered in the attack).

Prosecutors attempted to poke holes in Sheppard's testimony, and emphasize his extra-marital affair with Susan Harris, and the vagueness of his description. In return, Sheppard and his attorney were able to set up troubling details about an intense police interrogation of Sheppard that demonstrated the police settled on Sheppard as their *only* suspect—almost immediately.

Outside the courtroom, the trial continued to draw an unusual amount of attention across the nation, assisted in large part by the presence of several national reporters and columnists including Walter Winchell and Kilgallen.

Kilgallen, a reporter for Hearst newspapers, was a celebrity in her own right, having appeared since 1950 alongside Steve Allen, Soupy Sales and Arlene Francis as a regular panelist on the CBS primetime game show, *What's My Line?* Newspapers across the country carried Kilgallen's columns from the Sheppard trial, most of which focused more on the "circus" of the event rather than the actual proceedings.

Her opening day column was typical: "Dr. Sam Sheppard walked into the ugly small courtroom of his trial for murder today looking like a movie star playing the role of a defendant wrongly accused. All the correct emotions crossed his handsome face—tension, restraint, a conscious nobility of gaze, a kind of chin-up determination to face the unpleasantness without flinching."[133]

Just as her male counterparts focused attention on the physical appearance of Sheppard's paramour, Susan Harris, Kilgallen did likewise with the defendant.

"He is wide-shouldered and walks like an athlete, inches taller than most of the men in the courtroom. His face is sensual and a little spoiled looking, with the kind of spoiled look so often seen on the face of a man who cannot remember when was refused a dance or a kiss. His dress was equally appropriate for a murder trial or a cocktail party—the dark blue suit, soft white shirt, black knitted tie, black socks, black shoes. It made it easy for the spectator to visualize him in more casual moments."[134]

As he awaited the verdict in his cell on the upper floors of the courthouse, a photographer was permitted to capture an image of Sheppard gazing solemnly out the windows of the courts building to the street below.[135]

The jury of seven men and five women deliberated for 102 hours before the jury foreman who pressed a button in the deliberation room just after four p.m. on December 19, 1954, setting off a buzzer in the courtroom indicating a verdict had at last been reached.

As the verdict was read, Sheppard "leaned back in his chair. His eyes were closed. He was clinching his hands so tightly that his knuckles turned white."[136]

Despite Judge Blythin's stern warning that he would tolerate no displays of emotion or reaction to the verdict, as he read the jury's finding out loud, "We, the members of the jury, find the defendant not guilty of first-degree murder" gasps and exclamations arose from spectators in the jam-packed courtroom. "The judge paused, momentarily, apparently interrupted, and shot a sharp glance toward the back of the room. Then, he finished the sentence, 'but guilty of second-degree murder.' Sheppard had opened his eyes. He closed them again."[137]

Blythin wasted no time, he ordered Sheppard to rise and stand before the high bench. Asked if he had anything to say before sentence was pronounced, Sheppard said: "I would like to say here that I am not guilty and I feel there has been proof presented that has definitely proved I could not have performed this crime."[138]

Years of appeals would follow, most of them based on the assertion that Judge Blythin had allowed too much outside influence on the trial by refusing to sequester jurors until they began deliberations, and rejecting repeated concerns raised by defense attorneys about the conduct of reporters in the courthouse.

Blythin's conduct was itself put into question as reporters noted he appeared "star-struck" as he often stepped down from the bench during court breaks to chat and visit with reporters as well as television celebrity, Dorothy Kilgallen.[139]

Although aggressive in pursuing an appeal, Sheppard's attorneys faced an uphill battle. The Ohio Court of Appeals rejected Sheppard's appeal in July 1955. In November 1956, two years after his conviction, the US Supreme Court also refused to hear an appeal of the case.

As time passed, a variety of occurrences also made the appeal seem almost impossible. The trial judge, Judge Blythin, died in 1958 and Sheppard's attorney, William Corrigan, died in July 1961.

These were just the latest losses Sheppard faced—Sheppard's mother, Ethel, died of a self-inflicted gunshot wound just seventeen days after his original conviction. His father, Richard, also died less than a month later from complications of a stomach ulcer. His father-in-law, Thomas Reese, also died of suicide in February 1963.

With Corrigan deceased, the Sheppard family engaged brash defense attorney F. Lee Bailey to take over the appeals effort. In July 1964, a federal district court judge ruled that Sheppard had been denied a fair trial and he was released from prison, a decade after he first entered.[140]

An appeals court briefly held in 1965 that Sheppard

should not be released, and affirmed his conviction. The US Supreme Court ruled in the matter in June 1966 by declaring the atmosphere of Sheppard's 1954 trial as one resembling a "carnival" that likely produced jury bias.[141]

As a result, Ohio prosecutors refiled murder charges against Sheppard and opened a second trial at the Cuyahoga County Criminal Courts Building on October 24, 1966. The second trial would bear little resemblance to the first.

Judge Francis J. Talty signaled he intended the second Sheppard trial to be run as a tight arrangement. Talty "set up severe restrictions: news reporters could not use cameras or tape recorders in the courtroom or even employ sketch artists. They could not install teletypes or special phones on the second and third floors of the courthouse. . . . [Courthouse] seats would be distributed on a first-come, first-served basis."[142]

Completed in just four weeks, jurors returned a "not guilty" verdict for Sheppard on November 16, 1966 and he was promptly released from prison.

Multiple theories posited by authors and others connected to the case swirled in the decades since—and a third court proceeding in the matter (a wrongful imprisonment suit brought by Sam "Chip" Sheppard, Jr.) was opened in 1999. Ohio's state appeals and Supreme Court later ruled, in 2002, that Sheppard's son did not have proper standing under Ohio law to sue for the wrongful imprisonment of a family member.

Sheppard himself died on April 6, 1970, the result of liver cancer. He was 46. In the last year of his life Sheppard gave in to promoters and others who sought to exploit his fame—raising eyebrows for his debut as a "professional wrestler" under the name of Sam "The Killer" Sheppard for more than forty matches.[143]

Confidential Matters On Trial

LOS ANGELES COUNTY HALL OF JUSTICE

August-October 1957—Los Angeles, California

The curtain rises today on what may be Hollywood's most star-studded production or on what might turn out to be a turkey that never got off the ground," *The Times* intoned on opening day of a trial in August 1957.[144]

The trial opened in Department forty-one in the Los Angeles County Hall of Justice, but was eventually moved to Department forty-three for space considerations.[145] The Hall of Justice, opened in 1925, held the growing county's courts for several decades until a new Los Angeles County Courthouse opened in 1958 (well-known because of its frequent appearances on TV and in films).

In the autumn of 1957, the Hall of Justice was hardly a place to find celebrities, though lines of fans lined up for the opening day of the libel and obscenity trial for defendants Fred and Marjorie Meade and their company, Hollywood Research, Inc., and Robert Harrison, the publisher of *Confidential* and *Whisper* magazines (and Marjorie Meade's uncle).

Confidential magazine had been a big success—circulation topping out at more than 14 million readers at one point. It prompted a series of competitors including *Dynamite, Exposed, Fame, Hush-Hush, Inside Story, The Low Down, On the Q. T., Private Lives, Tip Off, Top Secret, Uncensored,* and *Whisper.*[146]

In his opening statement for the trial, Assistant Attorney General Clarence Linn said the editors and writers of *Confidential* and *Whisper* magazines "would pick up a slip from the straight and narrow of an individual and depict it as a way of life."[147]

He alleged that the magazine's publishers and editors used women as lures "to tempt men into compromising situations and then reported them." Linn said that testimony would show that the Meade's "bought stories from people of the night life, questionable characters, private detectives" and that the "announced purpose of setting up Hollywood Research, Inc. was to form a cover-up operation."[148]

The Meade's operated Hollywood Research, Inc. as an investigative agency to dig up dirt on stars, the state contended. The Meade's said the company existed simply to verify "facts" reported to them by various story sources.

"We will show that the printed material was lewd and obscene, that it had a substantial tendency to corrupt and that an attempt was made to impeach the honesty and integrity of living persons," Linn proclaimed.[149]

Prosecutors accused the publishers of "printing ancient and forgotten sins dredged up from the gutters and blown into fanciful tales" while the defense contended that "the real stories behind the stories printed in *Confidential* are far worse than the actual stories in the magazine and the evidence will show it."[150]

Defense attorney Arthur J. Crowley said he planned to call celebrities to the stand to ask them directly whether the stories were correct or not.

"There was no intent here to crucify any individual for one slip off the straight and narrow," Crowley said. "There was never any desire by anyone to injury anybody." He said some of the articles were actually ones serving a public service, such as "Don't Take Those Abortion Pills"[151]

"Scores of Hollywood figures are on two-hour notice to appear as witnesses but there is little likelihood any of them will be seen in court until the defense goes into action," the UPI reported.[152]

Linn accused Crowley of making reference to calling as many as 100 stars to the stand as an attempt to launch "a reign of terror" to cause the state to dismiss the case, but that stars would be called as needed. "Hollywood does not control justice in California," Linn declared.[153]

Heartthrob actor Tab Hunter was one of those unable to stop a subpoena and was photographed seated outside the courtroom, but his attorney Henry Weiss was successful in keeping him off the witness stand. Hunter had reason to steer clear. In September 1955, *Confidential* had printed details about his 1950 arrest at an alleged all-male sex party in Los Angeles County—a criminal incident the aspiring actor had prayed no one would ever know.

Writing about the story decades later—and after he had publicly acknowledged his homosexuality—Hunter said "I had been arrested for disorderly conduct when police raided a party at which I — and a number of other gay people — were in attendance. *Confidential* then ran the story on its cover and described it as 'a pajama party,' insinuating that it had been some sort of gay orgy."[154]

Weiss, known as an attorney who "specialized in the massaging of arrests of homosexuals in Los Angeles,"[155] also represented actor Rory Calhoun. Calhoun was issued a subpoena but never called to appear in the case.[156]

Both Hunter and Calhoun were eventually understood to be lower-level stars sacrificed to save a closeted homosexual "A" list star, Rock Hudson. One version of events suggests that Hollywood agent Henry Willson, who represented both Calhoun, Hunter *and* Hudson, willingly fed details of Hunter's past to *Confidential* editors (along with cash) to protect Hudson from being revealed as gay.[157]

The state submitted stories from *Confidential* that they claimed were libelous and/or obscene, involving among others Frank Sinatra, Maureen O'Hara, Dick Powell, June Allyson, Robert Mitchum, Tab Hunter, Dorothy Dandridge, Mae West, and Liberace.

The Independent newspaper in Long Beach, California—didn't hold back in its coverage of the trail. For its August 15, 1957 edition, *The Independent* ran a banner headline that promised "Stars' 'Sex Orgy' Stories Read in Court" above publicity photos of Sinatra, West, Mitchum, troubadour Eddie Fisher, and silver screen bombshell Jayne Mansfield, Swedish actress Anita Ekberg, and French temptress Corinne Calvet.[158]

Judge Herbert V. Walker seemed to surprise prosecutors by accepting a cardboard box full of back issues of *Confidential* and *Whisper* magazines, but then asking that the relevant articles be read aloud into the court record. Deputy Attorney General William L. Ritzi seemed reluctant to do so, telling the judge, "It might take two or three days to read them."[159]

Walker insisted the articles be read out loud. "Ritzi sighed" and "looked grimly at the wall clock and picked up the first magazine" to read.[160]

Independent staff writer Bob Houser wrote that "One could hear a pin drop in the crowded Los Angeles courtroom Wednesday as . . . Ritzi took the witness stand with a pile of *Confidential* and *Whisper* magazines and began reading spicy stories about Hollywood celebrities."[161]

Ritzi read "sex-saturated stories" from thirteen separate issues of the magazines, "sometimes stumbling over the purplish phrasing and tricky word play of lurid pieces."[162]

At times snickering and giggling among spectators in the audience caused Judge Walker to reissue his request for restraint. He also ordered anyone under the age of eighteen removed from the courtroom. "We'll have no laughing in the courtroom," Walker warned.[163]

The LA Times described the reading of the magazines by Ritzi in dramatic language as well: "*Confidential* magazine's dog-eared back numbers blew open like a Pandora's box in court here yesterday allowing mischievous details of Hollywood gossip to escape into the public record."[164]

They noted Ritzi read the accounts "with painful reluctance" from a cardboard box full of magazines and noted that "actual reading of the allegedly libelous stories into the record apparently open the door for a prolonged wraps-off, name-naming trial of the magazine and their associates."[165]

Labeled "People's Exhibit Thirteen," Ritzi read the *Confidential* article about O'Hara's alleged sexual encounter in a back row at Hollywood's famous Grauman's Chinese Theatre. The article, titled, "It Was the Hottest Show in Town When Maureen O'Hara Cuddled in Row Thirty-Five," alleged that O'Hara and an unnamed "handsome, tall Latin-American escort" were spread across three seats in the theater. "She was in the darndest position to watch a movie," the article read. "As far as she was concerned, it was double feature night and she was giving away more than dishes."[166]

Another line in the story read with particular emphasis by Ritzi asserted: "Even the usher in Grauman's Theatre was shocked when he turned his flashlight on Maureen and her Latin boyfriend."[167]

O'Hara had been a key witness before the Los Angeles County grand jury that brought the original indictments in the case, and the Meade's through their attorneys continued to assert they could produce eyewitnesses to verify the story.

Eventually Ritzi's voice began to fail him after reading thousands of words out loud, and Deputy AG Linn spelled him.

Among the other stories read were ones alleging that Dandridge had taken a male paramour into the woods at a Lake Tahoe resort for the purpose of having sex in the great outdoors; that Sinatra ate bowls of Wheaties cereal between multiple sexual encounters with a showgirl to keep his stamina up; Fisher engaged in a sex orgy with three women at a Detroit hotel; Mansfield hosting her personal security guard for overnight sexual trysts at her California home; the alleged propensity of Mitchum to strip naked at parties; purported nymphomaniac tendencies of Calvet and Egbert; and suggestions that West had a penchant for "Negro boxers" and other African-American men as sex partners.[168]

Outside the courtroom, defense attorney Crowley vowed that they would produce eyewitnesses to the O'Hara story—"There were a lot of people in Grauman's Chinese Theatre that night," he said. Pressed by reporters, Crowley added that his eyewitnesses "will not be ladies of the night, either" referring to the apparent impeachment of other defense witnesses.[169]

Some stars were frightened and pressured studio bosses to flex political muscle to keep their names out of the affair. But others were ready to fight back. Hollywood film legend Errol Flynn, who had won a suit against *Confidential* in previous years, told reporters in New York that he was eager to come to the defense of his fellow actors.

"I think it is about time someone stepped forward to unsully the fair names of we Thespians," Flynn said. "If someone wants to hear from me, I'll be more than anxious to open my trap. It seems to me that all of us have done certain things at some time that we are not happy about. I insist that actors are no different than anyone else. But the fact that this magazine is getting away with a pack of lies is an outrage against civil liberties."[170]

Fellow actor David Wayne also joined in: "There is no one's life, if completely exposed, that wouldn't show a little unfortunate background" and said that *Confidential* and *Whisper* magazines engaged in "a blackmail of a rather sickening form."[171]

As the Meade's left the courtroom for the first day, an attorney for O'Hara served them with a subpoena for a one-million-dollar libel suit. Liberace was also suing them for $25 million.[172] Dandridge pursued a two-million-dollar suit of her own, filed in a Fort Worth, Texas court.[173]

After the first day of proceedings, a disappointed writer for the Associated Press reported, "There were lights and cameras, but little action Friday as the curtain went up on the criminal libel cases involving *Confidential* magazine and a long list of Hollywood personalities. Any self-respecting movie producers would have been aghast at sending a star-studded attraction to such a limping start."[174]

"While an eager public jammed the courtroom and the corridors leading to it, hoping for spicy details of the private lives of movie stars, the case almost got lost in a maze of legal technicalities."[175]

Outside of court, actor and television bigwig Desi Arnaz denied he had a Palm Springs affair with a forty-one-year-old "admitted prostitute" Ronnie Quinlan in October 1944 during a period in which he was briefly separated from his wife, Lucille Ball. Quinlan had been paid $1,500 by *Confidential* for her version of the story, and said her affair with Arnaz occurred in 1944 during an "interlocutory divorce" by Desi and Lucy, but the couple later reconciled before launching their hit CBS television series, "*I Love Lucy.*"[176]

Reporters reached Arnaz at the Del Mar race track and he confirmed he had read the *Confidential* story when it was published, and declared it "a lot of baloney. I don't remember meeting the lady and I guess I'm being kind calling her a lady. I was in the Army in 1944 and I think I was somewhere up north. I don't remember being in Palm Springs. From the pictures I've seen of her, Mrs. Quinlan, I don't think I could have done anything like that."[177]

Quinlan openly admitted under questioning from defense attorneys that she was "engaged in prostitution." Reporters noted, "Her appearance as the day's chief prosecution witness was the high spot of the session. She showed up wearing a snug white-knit sleeveless sheath with a high-cut V-neck. She wore her orange hair loose and it reached several inches beneath her shoulders."[178]

Los Angeles Times reporter Jack Jones (later a Pulitzer Prize winner) was less friendly in his description of Quinlan, noting that "her faced is stretched with the hardened lines of too many nights in Hollywood" and referring to her hair as "dyed and dry" and her appearance looking "tired."[179]

Quinlan said the Arnaz story, as printed by *Confidential*, "stuck to the truth as I know it."

Quinlan said she made many suggestions for stories, but only two were ever published—the one about an alleged affair with Arnaz and another about Herb Jeffries, a "Negro" actor and jazz singer to whom she was once married.

She testified that "Mr. Harrison told me he was primarily interested in the sexual activities of the movie stars. He told me that the more lewd and lascivious a story, the more colorful the magazine." She said Harrison often pressured her for "stories and tips about rendezvous with celebrities."[180]

Small-time Hollywood writers and detectives testified of being paid for researching tips provided by Quinlan and others and that Harrison even asked whether audio wire taps could be established to verify information.

The prosecution ended its case with testimony from film producer Paul Gregory who said that Marjorie Meade had requested a payment of $800 to $1,000 in order to "kill" a damaging story for *Confidential* about Gregory, and actors Mitchum, Charles Laughton and Elsa Lanchester.

"Mrs. Meade broke down in tears after the Gregory testimony" and took to the stand to deny she had ever met or talked to Gregory.[181] So overcome with emotion, a doctor was summoned for the defendant and the judge allowed a three-hour recess for Mrs. Meade to gather her emotions.[182]

True to their promise, defense attorneys opened their case with alleged eyewitnesses to the reported O'Hara tete-a-tete inside the Grauman's Chinese Theatre in November 1953. James Craig, a British born film producer who claimed he was employed as assistant manager of the theatre, confirmed he was paid $200 as the source of the information in the *Confidential* article.

He said, "The flame-haired actress and a man described as a Mexican entered the theatre at 10:30 p.m. and were seated in the back row," the AP's Bob Thomas reported. "Later, he declared, an usher asked him to investigate the couple and Craig ultimately asked them to leave."[183]

Craig testified, "Miss O'Hara was lying across seats and over his lap. . . . She was disheveled, very untidy. . . . When I observed what was going on, I coughed, but they did nothing at all." He said he then went to retrieve a flashlight and when he returned and shined it on the couple, "they suddenly jumped to attention and returned to their seats."[184]

He further testified that an usher again told him "they were at it again" and he said he found both of them occupying one seat, seated face-to-face. "This time I flashed the light on them and told them politely to leave," Craig said.[185]

The theater manager's detailed testimony included a claim that the famous actress asked to borrow his flashlight in order to find a diamond cufflink that had fallen from her Latin escort's jacket.

In case the detailed testimony was not enough, Judge Walker allowed an in-court demonstration of how O'Hara and her date were allegedly seated in the theatre. "[Craig] and a buxom newspaperwoman [Lee Belser], who volunteered her services, twisted themselves in three courtroom seats while judge, jury and spectators watched in fascination," the *Los Angeles Times* shared. The judge "glowered sternly over the courtroom, his ears attuned to titters, ready to rap down with his gavel. He had warned that he would let the show go on, but let no one think it was a comedy."[186]

Under cross examination, Craig was asked why he supplied the article to the gossip magazine and he offered the explanation that "I wanted it made public that a public figure should behave in such a manner" and then added, "The incident was humorous, but at the same time, it left a bad taste in my mouth. I didn't like it."[187]

Prosecutors later produced Craig's former boss, Ralph Hathaway, the manager of Grauman's Chinese Theatre, who said Craig was a doorman, but never an assistant manager and that he had never reported any such incident to the theater's management.[188]

Jurors, in messages to the judge, expressed confusion about the semantics of the O'Hara encounter, and requested a visit to the theater in person.

As unusual as the case had already been, Judge Walker approved the request and escorted jurors, court reporters, attorneys for both sides, and the defendants in a bus to the theater located about seven miles across town at 6925 Hollywood Boulevard. Before departing the Los Angeles Hall of Justice, Walker "admonished the jurors that they must talk to nobody during the trip and inspection."[189]

Disgusted by the claims emanating from the courtroom in Los Angeles, O'Hara amended her libel suit against the magazine seeking three million dollars in damages, instead of one million dollars. She also told reporters, through a publicist, that her passport would prove she was in Spain in November 1953 making a film when the alleged sexual encounter occurred in the movie theater.[190]

To make her case even further, O'Hara willingly appeared in court (along with Dandridge) to testify against the magazine owners and forcefully answered shouted questions from reporters outside the courtroom about the alleged affair.

Oscar and Golden Globe-nominated Dandridge told the court that the article about her alleged "outdoor" liaison with a white man outside a Lake Tahoe resort in 1950 was impossible. She said "restrictions on Negroes" at Lake Tahoe made such a meeting impossible: "I was never alone with [the white man]. I never took a walk in the woods with him or alone. I never took a ride with him."[191]

She said she strictly observed the resort's rules that Negroes could not patronize with white staff or guests: "There was no choice about it. I stayed in my suite most of the time. I worked nights [singing in the showroom] and slept in the afternoon."[192]

O'Hara repeated her claims that she was not in the United States on the date alleged for the incident at the theater, although she acknowledged she had a social friendship with Mexican businessman Enrique Parra and had went to nightclubs and restaurants with him in the past.

O'Hara said she had never been at Grauman's Chinese Theatre other than for "film premieres when I was accompanied by members of my family." She glared at a defense attorney who questioned her about having Mexican friends. "I have very many good friends that are Mexican," she said.[193]

Reporters didn't miss the fact that O'Hara and Dandridge, the only two major stars who appeared at the trial, had stolen the spotlight.

"Miss O'Hara's dramatic entrance into the trial that has virtually come to center on her instead of on the defendants, Fred and Marjorie Meade and *Confidential* and Whisper magazines, came minutes after jurors returned from looking over Grauman's Chinese Theatre."[194]

O'Hara capped her testimony by nearing tears when she said she had been offered no significant acting roles since the *Confidential* article appeared and that her young daughter "cried herself to sleep" about the stories and resulting rumors.[195]

Activities outside the courtroom continued to be as interesting as those inside the court. Defense attorneys threatened they would produce Enrique Parra to verify the story about O'Hara, emphasizing that he was married to another women. Parra was never called as a witness, however.

The prosecution's "star witness," prostitute Ronnie Quinlan (described by *The Los Angeles Times* as a "Hollywood playgirl") made news of her own after suffering facial injuries and a broken tooth in a domestic dispute with her estranged twenty-one-year-old husband as the trial progressed. Quinlan reported she was beaten with a whisky bottle inside her motel room in Hollywood Heights.[196]

Further adding to the intrigue, two potential witnesses died while the trial was underway. Polly Gould, a former investigator employed by *Confidential* magazine, was found dead in her apartment of an apparent overdose, while middleweight boxer Albert "Chalky" Wright, one of Mae West's alleged lovers, died in a bathtub drowning accident.[197]

As the trial dragged on into six weeks, and as reporters noted, "In the absence of the stars themselves [O'Hara and Dandridge notwithstanding], the trial has developed into a name-dropping spree of fabulous proportions." Jurors would find "famed personalities as only shadowy figures from the pages of the magazine. As the sensational case moves toward its climatic scene, the jurors have yet to see or hear . . . [a lot of] movie stars."[198]

When finally presented the case, jurors set a new California record for the length of their deliberations and finally gave up on October 1, 1957. Prosecutors then announced they would accept a settlement option from the Meade's and their company to pay a fine for articles that may have violated obscure California business codes.

The magazine's publishers eventually settled a variety of civil suits pending against the publications, and under the settlement agreement with the state, moved the magazines toward more consumer or public affairs reporting. With celebrity sex and gossip stories gone, the magazines floundered and *Confidential* eventually folded.

One More Big Trial for "Old Red"

DALLAS COUNTY COURTHOUSE

March 1964—Dallas, Texas

Photo courtesy of Robert and Billye Duncan Bultman

By March 1964, the Dallas County Courthouse—known by locals as "Old Red" for its red sandstone exterior walls—was nearing the end of its life as the center of justice in the "big D."

Already under construction across the street was a new modern office building that would replace the aging 1892 structure that was actually the sixth courthouse on the parcel donated to the city in pioneer days. Bounded by Houston, Main, Commerce and Market streets, the courthouse faced the city's modern Dealey Plaza to the west.

Before "Old Red" could be retired to other less glamorous uses, it played host to the strange and noteworthy murder trial of Jack L. Ruby.

While the Ruby trial once again drew worldwide attention to Dallas, there was little question what the outcome of the murder trial of Ruby would be. After all, Ruby *had* stepped from the sidelines in the basement of the Dallas Police Department on Sunday morning, November 24, 1963 and plunged his .38 caliber handgun into the abdomen of a handcuffed Lee Harvey Oswald, accused Presidential assassin, and fired a fatal shot.

NBC broadcast the Oswald shooting live—CBS and ABC were showing preparations for the state funeral of President John F. Kennedy in Washington, D. C. and joined the Oswald assassination as his dying, gray body was being loaded into an ambulance. Eventually an estimated 180 million Americans had witnessed the murder either live, or in repeated slow motion moments after it occurred.

NBC News reporter Tom Petit was among those crammed into the crowded police station garage. As Ruby fired his single shot, Petit yelled into his microphone, "He's been shot! He's been shot! Lee Oswald has been shot!"[199]

Petit described the scene as "absolute panic" and that "pandemonium has broken out."[200]

Ruby's act was startling but melded quickly into a surreal forty-eight hours in Dallas that had started on Friday afternoon, November 22, 1963. On that day, just after 12:30 p.m. Central time, the nation's thirty-fifth President, John F. Kennedy, was assassinated as he rode in an open limousine motorcade through Dealey Plaza in downtown Dallas.

Later that day Dallas Police cornered and arrested the twenty-four-year-old Oswald inside the Texas Theatre, about three miles southwest of where President Kennedy was slain (and where Texas Governor John Connally was critically wounded).

Oswald, a misfit former Marine and native of New Orleans, had settled in Dallas in the months after he returned from the Soviet Union with his Russian bride. He had previously attempted to defect to Russia, but eventually returned to the US, but maintained his highly pro-Communist political viewpoints.

Oswald's path crossed with Ruby, born into a Jewish Chicago family as Jacob Leonard Rubenstein (a name he later shortened to Ruby in December 1947), as Ruby and all Americans attempted to take in the reality that President Kennedy had been murdered. Ruby's friends and co-workers all reported he was singularly distraught over Kennedy's assassination, an event he learned about as he ordered display advertisements at *The Dallas Morning News* when the news broke of shots being fired just five blocks down South Houston Street.

Ruby, the product of a troubled and embattled childhood, grew up in Jewish and Italian slums in Chicago and was drafted into World War II by the US Army. He returned from the war to his home in Chicago, but by 1947 he had cashed out of a novelty manufacturing venture with his brothers, and relocated to Dallas.

Once in Dallas, Ruby joined with his sister Eva Grant in making important connections to various dance hall and nightclub operations in some of the rougher neighborhoods of Dallas. It was just his latest attempt to "make it" as a businessman—seemingly the only thing that mattered to Ruby. While popular with women, he never married or demonstrated any interest in having a family.

Ruby and his sister took over operation of the Singapore Supper Club and renamed it the Silver Spur, but it still was well known as a night club "frequented by young toughs," and later acquired the Vegas Club, known for its female strippers.

Over time, Ruby's main source of income was the operation of the night clubs and dance halls in Dallas.

By 1963, Ruby had shed the Silver Spur and held interest in two other nightclubs, the Vegas Club and the Carousel Club. The Carousel Club, originally known as the Sovereign Club, was one of three "burlesque clubs" in downtown Dallas and served champagne, beer, ribs and pizza. "The Carousel generally employed four [female] strippers, a master of ceremonies, an assistant manager, a band, three or four waitresses, and a porter or handyman," the Warren Commission investigation of the JFK assassination reported. "Net receipts averages about $5,000 per month, most of which was allocated to the club's payroll."[201]

Both the Carousel and Vegas clubs were known as "adult entertainment" establishments, the Carousel frequently advertising its strip shows in local newspapers.

Ruby viewed the Carousel Club located at 1312 ½ Commerce Street in downtown Dallas as "a better class joint with better people"[202] and touted it as "a fucking classy joint." As *Texas Monthly* magazine noted, Ruby's move downtown had been a smart one, situating his club close to established restaurants and hotels.[203]

"Jack Ruby ran what he considered a 'decent' place, a 'high-class' place, a place that Dallas could view with pride," journalist Gary Cartwright wrote. "'Punks' and 'characters' who wandered in by mistake were as likely to leave with an impression of Jack Ruby's fist where their nose used to be. Cops and newspapermen, that's who Ruby wanted in his place. Dallas cops drank there regularly, and none of them ever paid for a drink."[204]

One former business associate, Dallas real estate agent Joseph Rossi, described Ruby as "a tough, extremely emotional character who wanted recognition, social recognition, more than anything in this world." Rossi said Ruby, known to be blunt with those he disliked (and even physically abusive with some of the female strippers in his clubs) was also "patriotic, very emotional. If someone said anything bad about the President, instead of discussing things calmly, Jack would probably sock the guy," Rossi shared.[205]

Ruby, well-known to Dallas Police vice squad detectives, had followed closely the events of the Kennedy assassination. Just hours after the event, he tearfully told employees at the Carousel Club that it would not open that night out of respect to the slain President.

His familiarity with police meant Ruby easily gained access to the basement of the Dallas Police Department headquarters at 106 South Harwood Street by entering through the Commerce Street ramp to the underground garage. There he joined dozens of reporters and other onlookers watching as detectives prepared to transfer Oswald from the police department to the nearby Dallas County Jail.

As he emerged in front of a bank of cameras, Oswald looked drawn and tired—subjected to more than twelve hours of questioning by detectives—and what he claimed was physical abuse at the hands of police interrogators. As he left the office of Dallas Police Captain J. Will Fritz, head of the homicide division, Oswald was handcuffed to homicide detective James R. Leavelle. It was standard operating procedure.

Literally overrun by local and national television, radio and newspaper reporters in the hours following President Kennedy's assassination, "standard operating procedure" at the Dallas Police Department indicated the police had lost control of their own building. In the growing crowd, Ruby posed as a reporter and attended a jam-packed news conference on the night of the JFK assassination. No one questioned his presence, it seemed, though he later told Warren Commission investigators that he was armed during the police headquarters media scrum as well.[206]

As Ruby's trial approached in early 1964, it was as the presiding Judge Joe B. Brown, Sr. later wrote, "the surrogate [trial] for the trial Lee Harvey Oswald would never face."[207] Even before the trial began, pre-trial hearings at the Dallas County Courthouse made headlines. In a failed attempt to gain bond to be released from the county jail until his trial, a December 23, 1963 hearing was highlighted by the appearance of one of Ruby's employees, a nineteen-year-old stripper named Karen Lynn Bennett (known on stage as "Little Lynn").

Searched by a female bailiff, "Little Lynn" said she came to court with the unloaded pistol in her purse by accident—having forgotten that it was there.[208] "During this hearing and the balance of the proceedings, Sheriff [William F.] Decker searched every person who entered the courtroom. He was, I think, justifiably afraid that some person might attempt to take the life of Ruby."[209]

"Little Lynn" was promptly relieved of her gun, removed from the courtroom, and held briefly on a $1,000 bond. The incident with "Little Lynn" was but "a foretaste of things to come during the trial," Judge Brown later wrote.[210]

Her shenanigans also overshadowed the testimony of Detective Leavelle who was handcuffed to Oswald as he was shot. Leavelle said Ruby "looked as calm [on the day of Oswald's shooting] as he did in court Monday, completely at ease." Defense attorneys attempted to portray Ruby as an emotional, excited man on the day of the shooting and failed in both getting a bond set for Ruby, and getting the case moved from Dallas on a change of venue motion.[211]

The colorful Melvin Belli, a noted San Francisco attorney who flew to Dallas to take up Ruby's cause at the center of the spotlight, seemed to be setting the stage for a conspiracy theory alleging that Ruby was used to eliminate Oswald, or failing that, to cast Ruby as so diminished by his emotions that he lacked the ability to premediate the murder. In court, Belli pestered police witnesses with provocative, leading questions such as "You as a Texan felt angry and agitated toward Oswald, didn't you?"[212] District Attorney Henry Wade won repeated objections to try and quell Belli's intense questioning.

Witnesses called by Belli included Ruby's roommate, George Senate, who testified that Ruby was "highly agitated" on the Sunday morning he left their apartment to go to the Dallas Police headquarters. He said there was "a difference in his facial expression, in the nervousness of his talk, his pacing forth and back—it just wasn't Jack."[213]

For his part, Ruby appeared either tired, bored or amused, depending upon who was testifying.

The dank hallways of the aging courthouse were crammed full of reporters from across the world, including some who had set up temporary teletype machines on tables in order to broadcast details from the case against Ruby. Judge Brown, concerned that his regular courtroom included a gallery that seated only sixty-four people, agreed to have the case moved to a larger room in the courthouse.

"Most of those I saw [in the courtroom] were the usual courthouse hangers-on who attend all trials," Judge Brown said. "But I did spot a few courthouse employees who had slipped away from their jobs for a moment to watch this event."[214]

The bail hearing was a perfunctory affair after the incident with "Little Lynn"—the judge had no intention of releasing Ruby. Ruby was held during the proceedings in a small room behind the judge's bench in the courthouse, and more permanently in a cell on the upper floors of the courthouse.

The circus atmosphere of Ruby's trial carried over to the sidewalk outside "Old Red." There a man and woman picketed carrying signs that read, "A Person Who Does Wrong is Not Insane" and "Psychiatry Is Not the Hope of Killers."[215]

Judge Brown was unconcerned about the picketers—potential jurors for the Ruby trial had been kept away from them—but the arrival of Oswald's mother, Marguerite Oswald, did provide for excitement.

"[She] was outside the courtroom intending to enter as a spectator," Judge Brown recalled. "I had to do something about it. The danger was that she would create a scene in the courtroom in the presence of the jury, thus creating a mistrial. To prevent this, the state subpoenaed her as a witness" as she talked to reporters outside the courtroom. Once listed as a witness, she was not permitted to enter the courtroom until called.[216]

Brown also put his foot down at any suggestion that cameras be permitted in the courtroom for the Ruby trial. While acknowledging the case had naturally drawn worldwide attention, "the courtroom was where serious and continuous business was being conducted" and "inside the courtroom, a dignified trial could be conducted. But in the corridors [of the courthouse] and [in the] streets outside, where the court had no control, histrionic lawyers and exceptional events captured by the television cameras resembled a circus."[217]

The "rules" guiding the trial were also tough on jurors—each of them selected was required to be sequestered in drab eight-by-eight-foot "apartments" inside the courthouse until the conclusion of the proceedings.

"There are fourteen sleeping rooms in the [courthouse] dormitory," news reports indicated. "Twelve for the jury members and two for bailiffs. There is also a room for deliberation and one show room. The sleeping rooms contain a bed, wall toilet, wash bowl, and mirror. Only the bailiff's rooms have telephones."[218]

The deliberating room that would house jurors was only slightly less stark, it seems, with the addition of a sink and "a small stove for making coffee. At meal time, the jurors will be taken out to eat at a restaurant near the courthouse. None of the rooms in the dormitory on the ninth floor of the courthouse has windows."[219]

Ruby's defense attorneys, Belli and Joe Tonahill, openly complained to any reporters who would listen that it was impossible for their client to get a fair trial in Dallas. Taking their lunch outside the courthouse, the nearly adjacent Texas School Book Depository Building (from where investigators said Oswald had fired the fatal shots at the President) served as backdrop for their media interviews.

Reporters focused a lot on jury selection as Belli and Tonahill posed dozens upon dozens of objections about alleged bias from potential jurors. Their tactics wore thin, and eventually they relented and began to approve jurors after intense questioning.

"More than two hundred writers and cameramen are here," wrote *Kanas City Star* reporter Robert K. Sanford. "The hurly-burly consists of cameramen pointing lenses at anything that moves in the corridors outside the courtroom, and Miss Dorothy Kilgallen [a popular journalist better known for her appearances on the CBS game show "*What's My Line?*" than for her reporting] holding court in the courtroom for her TV admirers during recesses. Judge Brown was one of those who spoke to her at one of her sessions."[220]

State witnesses during the March 1964 trial resembled the cast for the preliminary hearing in December 1963. A parade of police officers testified to what they knew about Ruby, and what they witnessed on November twenty-four—when as many as seventy police officers stood by while Ruby shot Oswald.

Belli once again called Bennet, AKA "Little Lynn," one of Ruby's strippers who stole headlines in December. Now pregnant, the young woman said Ruby could be unpredictable and erratic, and was especially grieved by President Kennedy's death. She had seen Ruby that day as she borrowed twenty-five dollars to pay her rent.

"I like Jack as a friend," she told jurors, "but as a boss I never knew when he might blow up."[221]

As Bennett testified in the Ruby trial, seven prisoners housed in holding cells on the upper floors of the courthouse, took advantage of the hub-bub, fashioning a gun made out of a bar of soap, and attempted an escape. Two of them ended up outside the Ruby courtroom in front of live television cameras.

Judge Brown lamented the occurrences, labeling them "another sideshow that was to keep Dallas black in the eyes of people across the country."[222]

El Paso Herald-Post reporter Inez Robb was philosophical about the events: "If the Oswald slaying was the nation's first televised murder, then yesterday's fully televised jail break must have set some kind of record, too."[223]

After all the distractions the Ruby trial endured inside the old courthouse, the eight men and four women on the jury took just two hours and twenty-four minutes to return their expected verdict of guilty. The fifty-two-year-old Ruby sat silently as the verdict was read, and offered no comments as he was led from the courtroom. One of his sisters, Aileen Kaminsky ran from the courtroom in tears after hearing the verdict.

Outside the courtroom, Belli declared "This thing was the greatest kangaroo railroad in history" and declared Dallas was "a city of shame forever." He repeated his previous concerns that Ruby was not safe in the hands of Dallas County authorities.[224]

Not surprisingly, DA Henry Wade disagreed and said he was "well pleased" with the verdict which he called "totally warranted." He said the citizens of Dallas County should be proud that "lynch law" had played no role in the search for justice for the murder of "a helpless, manacled man."

"An innocent verdict would have put civilization back toward barbarity and lynch law," Wade added.[225]

The expressed concerns about Ruby's safety were not bore out. A month after his conviction, more than 100 prisoners on the seventh floor jail of the Dallas County Jail staged a mini-riot, but jailers successfully shielded Ruby from harm.[226]

On January 3, 1967, Ruby collapsed in his cell at the Dallas County Jail and was rushed to Parkland Memorial Hospital (the same hospital that treated both President Kennedy and Oswald). He was pronounced dead shortly after his arrival there, a coroner ruling he died of a pulmonary embolism as a side-effect to his increasingly debilitating lung cancer.[227]

Three years after Ruby's trial concluded, Dallas County courts moved from the "Old Red" courthouse to their new modern office building. "Old Red" was used as headquarters for the State Department of Public Welfare and family courts until 1990, when it was finally vacated. Following a twenty-three-million-dollar renovation, "Old Red" once again opened in 2007 (complete with a replaced clock tower) as the new home of the Dallas County Historical Museum.[228]

A Young Nurse Faces Down Evil

PEORIA COUNTY COURTHOUSE
February 1967—Peoria, Illinois

Photo courtesy of Bruce Wicks

Anyone who has ever heard about the crimes of Richard Benjamin Speck understands the type of evil some men possess and the danger they represent to others.

At the age of twenty-four, Curozon Amurao, a nursing student in the United States from the Philippines, somehow managed to survive the treacherous blood lust Speck unleashed on a townhouse full of nursing students on July 13, 1966. She survived to stand to ensure Speck paid the penalty for his crimes.

Her struggle for survival in 1966 played out inside a townhouse in the densely packed neighborhoods of Stony

Island and Calumet Heights on the near Southside of Chicago. There, inside the first in a row of non-descript units at 2319 East One-Hundredth Street, eight other young nursing students were brutally stabbed and strangled to death.

More than a year later, the Peoria County Courthouse, about 160 miles from the murder scene, provided Amurao another moment to survive, and ultimately thrive.

Known to friends as "Cora," Amurao came to the US from a tiny village on the island of Mindoro, forty-two miles south of the capital of the Philippines, Manilla. The American-Filipino educational exchange program promised opportunity to young women like Amurao seeking a new life back home.[229]

She was enrolled as a student nurse studying in a program of students at South Chicago Community Hospital, just a mile or so away from her townhouse. The three-year course offered the promise of a good job and good wages for the rest of their lives. To make nursing school possible, Amurao had accepted an invitation to join a financially strapped group of other nurses who shared the rent at the townhouse, where they also helped one another study. Of the nine young women who lived in the unit, six were Americans and three were Filipino—and all were seniors nearing the end of their student training at the hospital.[230]

The Filipino women were already considered registered nurses back in the Philippines, but were seeking a similar designation from the more rigorous and advanced American program. Of the 114 women enrolled in the Chicago program in 1966, thirty-eight were from the Philippines. At the time of the attack, the three Filipino women had only been in Chicago for two months.[231]

The names of the eight young women from the townhouse on East One-Hundredth Street—Gloria Davy, Suzanne Farris, Merlita Gargullo, Valentia Pasion, Mary Ann Jordan, Patricia

Matusek, Nina Schmale, and Pamela Wilkening—have all but been forgotten in the half century since their murders.

It seems it always was so—as famed *Life* magazine writer Loudon Wainwright, Jr. offered, the fate of the killer "takes over" the lives of the victims, "obscuring matters at least equally important, matters having to do with the quality of [the] victims and their abruptly ended lives. In the aftermath of the crime, the person of the killer takes on a grotesque reality while the victims fade into the background of tears and funeral flowers."[232]

But Amurao, through her survival and her bravery in the face of intense scrutiny and fear, helped bring justice for the eight women in a dramatic scene played out at the Peoria County Courthouse.

The trial for Richard Speck, then just twenty-five years old himself, opened on February 20, 1967 at the courthouse in Peoria where the case had been moved in a seemingly futile attempt to find a jury who hadn't heard of the crime. The atrocious slaying of eight young women had not only been ubiquitous news in Illinois, but across the nation.

Prosecutors seeking the death penalty for Speck had two major pieces of evidence they planned to present, Amurao's eyewitness account, and fingerprint evidence linking Speck to the murder scene. Included among their evidence was an elaborate scale model of the townhouse built at a cost of $6,000 by FBI experts for the trial.[233]

There was no question that if a trial ever had a "star" witness, the quiet nursing student from the Philippines was it. Held under protective security by police (including a stay at the personal home of the Peoria County Sheriff), Amurao battled her doubts and walked through a phalanx of photographers and onlookers to enter the Peoria County Courthouse.

Amurao, one of eight children born to a working class family, she was considered the over-achieving child of the family. Her nursing instructors back in the Philippines described her as not a brilliant student, but adaptable. One said, "She could adjust easily. She was calm and had a good presence of mind."[234]

Calmness and presence of mind likely saved Amurao's life.

Amurao would tell jurors about a horrifying night of torture and blood. Only once did she lose her composure, but quickly regained herself.

As *Bloomington Pantagraph* reporter Ray Manahan wrote, under questioning by Prosecutor William Martin, "Miss Amurao calmly rose, stepped down from the witness box and walked to the table where Speck and his attorneys were seated. Standing directly in front of Speck, not three feet away, Miss Amurao pointed at him saying, 'This is the man.' Speck, slouched in his chair, his face very white, regarded her unflinchingly."[235]

Prior to identifying Speck, Amurao told of an average evening at the townhouse, doing her laundry and visiting with the other women present. She said she locked the front door to the townhouse at about 10:30 p.m. as she prepared to retire, but did not check if the back door was locked.

At about eleven p.m. she said she was awakened by knocks on the door of the bedroom she shared with several other women. Climbing down from her bunkbed, Amurao said she unlocked the bedroom door "and saw a man standing there pointing a gun at her. The man had [pock] marks on his face, blondish hair combed back with some sticking up in the front, and was wearing dark clothes."[236]

She said the man asked, "Where are your companions?" and grabbed her by the forearm. The other women in the room at the time, fellow Filipino students Merlita Gargullo and Valentia Pasion went to a back bedroom as Speck ordered. Once there, however, the three women jumped into a small closet and attempted to hold the door shut for several minutes, Amurao said.

Moments later Speck returned holding one of her American housemates, Pamela Wilkening, at gunpoint and prompted Wilkening to tell the women, "You come out of the closet, and he is not going to hurt you."[237]

Speck eventually herded six women to sit on the bedroom floor (by this time having brought both Wilkening, Nina Schmale and Patricia Matusek into the room). Telling the women he wanted money to get to New Orleans, and promising he wouldn't hurt them, several of the women found their purses and gave Speck all the money they could find.

To her great misfortune, Gloria Davy returned from a date to the apartment at about this time (around 11:30 p.m.) and screamed as she encountered Speck on the second floor of the townhouse. Moments later, Speck cut up bed sheets in order to tie the hands and feet of the now seven hostages he had commandeered.

Amurao said Speck kept reassuring the women, "Don't be afraid. I'm not going to kill you." Amurao testified that Speck was close enough for her to smell a heavy scent of alcohol on his breath.[238]

Psychologists and crime experts have theorized that the women were so cooperative with Speck, even unto their own deaths, because of their training as nurses. Trained to work their way through even the most horrible and challenging situations, some of the women may have thought they could talk Speck out of assaulting or even killing the women. They had badly underestimated the evil Speck possessed.

Shockingly, Speck had missed two other women in the townhouse at the time—Mary Ann Jordan and Suzanne

Farris—who were sleeping in another second floor bedroom. Hearing the struggle when Speck strangled Wilkening in an adjoining room, the two women opened the bedroom door and were quickly overtaken from behind by Speck who also ordered them to the floor, and tied their hands and feet.

A strange, almost systematic tale followed in Amurao's account as Speck took the women one-by-one and either strangled or stabbed them to death. Based on the testimony, it appeared he also at least attempted to sexually assault the women and, curiously, stopped to wash his hands in a bathroom basin between each slaying.

As the number of women alive dwindled down to four, Amurao said they tried "to hide themselves among the three bunk beds in the large south bedroom. The effort failed for three of the women—each of them dragged out and murdered as Speck's blood lust continued to explode.[239]

Amurao said she could see Davy as the only other woman still alive—lying on a lower bunk nearby and watched as Speck removed her blue jeans and sexually assaulted her.

"Miss Amurao testified that she lowered her head, but could hear something being unzipped," news accounts revealed. "Raising her head, she saw Speck lying with Miss Davy [on the bed]."[240]

Reporters noted Amurao's emotions rose and she began to weep quietly for a few moments, unable to give any further details of the rape playing out in front of her

"When the noise from the [bed] springs stopped, [Amurao] looked up and saw that speck and Miss Davy were gone," and she chose this moment to "quickly crawl and slide under the bunk where Miss Davy had lain and lay hidden from sight by a blanket which hung over the edge of the bed." [241]

She reported Speck returned to the room and turned the light on, but did not discover her under the bunk. Although

Amurao testified earlier that Speck had counted the number of women present—a total of nine—he apparently forgot his count and left with just eight of the women slain.

Speck's defense attorney, Gerald W. Getty, attempted to cross-examine Amurao, but the young woman was highly sympathetic to anyone who listened to her horrifying story. Getty focused briefly on whether Amurao had been led by police to identify Speck as the killer, but made little headway. Likewise, his questions about police procedures in collecting fingerprint evidence were not fruitful.

Prior to trial Getty had successfully argued for the transfer of the case from Cook County to another venue—Peoria, Illinois. The judge making the decision said he chose Peoria because it was far enough away from Chicago TV and radio stations to assist in finding an objective pool of jurors.[242]

Cook County Criminal Court Judge Herbert C. Paschen, who presided over the trial in Peoria County, set a tight set of rules for the proceedings, openly citing concerns about the shooting that took Lee Harvey Oswald's life in 1963 before he could face trial for killing President Kennedy. The judge restricted press coverage in particular, drawing (at least initially) complaints from the powerful *Chicago Tribune* and others.[243]

Among the restrictions ordered by Paschen was a rare "gag order" that forbid either prosecutors or defense attorneys, along with police or other court officials from giving "any leads, information or statements relative to the trial." The judge reserved the front three rows in the courtroom for the media, but required credentials for each.

Another rule limited movement in and out of the courtroom to only those times court is recessed or adjourned, "except in the case of emergency" the *Chicago Tribune's* William Jones reported. "No cameras or electronic equipment will be permitted in the courthouse. Sketches or drawings will not be allowed in the courthouse. All approaches to the courtroom and offices in the building must be kept clear. The Sheriff of Peoria County will search everyone entering the courtroom."[244]

The Peoria County Sheriff's Department seemed up to the task at hand, engaging an elaborate plan each day to move Speck from the adjacent county jail (by automobile) to the courthouse. Speck's egress to the courthouse was via private areas and so no media or members of the public could see him.

Cook County Sheriff's Department officials were equally cautious, refusing to tell reporters when Speck was to be transported the 160 miles to Peoria for trial (and later confirming they had done so under the cover of night via a state and local police convoy).

Eventually some of the rules were relaxed or reduced after media challenges were heard—including allowing a courtroom sketch artist and the publishing of the names and background information on the seven men and five women selected for the jury. Reporters later did report the jurors ranged in age from twenty-nine to seventy years old.[245]

Even with the strict restrictions in place, courtroom seats for media and observers from the general public were highly coveted. "They start lining up at 7:30 in the morning," a Peoria police officer told reporters about curious residents who wanted to see the trial.[246]

Not surprisingly, most of the onlookers wanted to see Speck in person, and hear the testimony of Amurao. "Most of the spectators are surprised at the security invoked throughout the courthouse for the trial," *The Chicago Tribune* shared.[247]

Spectators wanting a seat had to wait in line outside the courthouse first, then were admitted inside for a body search (including purses for women). Two female bailiffs were enlisted to help in searching the long line of courthouse "guests" each day.

One of the county's security guards, apparently trying to follow the judge's gag order, did tell a reporter that "Some of the spectators, particularly lawyers who work in the [courthouse] each day object to being searched. But I just remind them that about a week ago one of the women bailiffs even searched a nun."[248]

One group of hopeful spectators was absolutely turned away—high school students who used the bus transfer stop in front of the courthouse each day slipped into the building hoping to get a glimpse of the spectacle playing out in their town. They were immediately turned away, however, since the judge's order prohibited anyone under the age of eighteen from being present in the courtroom.[249]

Speck's defense was feeble, a parade of character witnesses (mostly his mother and sisters) seemed to confirm what was already known—Speck was an aimless, drunken loser who took advantage of others and disrespected women. Speck's mother, Margaret Speck Lindberg of Dallas, Texas, shed no tears about the fate facing her son, and testified essentially only to the fact that Speck was born and his father died when he was six years old. She blew a kiss to her son as she exited the courtroom, prompting an inappropriate smile on her son's face.[250]

As jurors deliberated the case, Judge Paschen loosed up on the courtroom rules and photographers quickly zeroed in on Speck as he sat in the courtroom cursing them. "Hey judge! Come here!" Speck yelled at one point to Paschen asking that the photographers be removed. "You're not going to let those newspaper guys take my picture are you? I don't want no pictures," Speck said.[251]

Awaiting sentencing, Speck was returned briefly to the Cook County Jail in Chicago. There, the psychiatrist employed by the Cook County Sheriff, Dr. Marvin Ziporyn, ran afoul of authorities as he began releasing details of his conversations with the killer. Promptly fired by the sheriff for his disclosures, Ziporyn went forward with plans to write his own book about the case.[252]

Speck himself made headlines as he gloated to a reporter from United Press International that he had witnessed opportunities to escape custody while he was being held in Peoria for his trial that lasted eight weeks.

"I could have grabbed a pistol which the guards kept holstered, but I didn't see what I would gain," Speck said. "I even told the guards that they shouldn't turn their backs because they might get hurt by some prisoner, but not by me."[253]

Cook County Sheriff Joseph I. Woods had had enough and ordered his own "gag order" on sheriff's department and jail personnel, declaring that "No information about anything Speck paints, eats, or whether he sleeps during the day is to be released.[254]

On June 5, 1967, under heavy guard of ten officers Peoria, Cook County and Illinois State Police officers, Speck was taken back to the Peoria County Courthouse to hear Judge Paschen sentence him to death. During the brief hearing, Speck did not speak as Paschen announced "The body of Richard Speck is to become the custody of the warden at the Joliet Penitentiary and on the day of September 1, 1967, he shall be put to death by electrocution."[255]

During the hearing, reporters noted Speck "looked disinterested but for a moment turned his eyes from Judge Paschen's face and looked back at the rows of occupants in the crowded courtroom. He cast a contemptuous look at some of the relatives of the murdered girls and then his gaze once again rested on the judge."[256]

Gloria Davy's father, Charles Davy, attended most of the court proceedings and was the unofficial spokesman for the surviving families. He told reporters, "We hope the judgment of the jury and the court will be carried out as speedily as possible.[257]

Outside the courthouse, all Speck would say to reporters is "You can't win 'em all," as he was shoved inside a police car.[258]

On June 29, 1971, the US Supreme Court reversed the death penalty sentence given to Speck (along with thirty-eight other condemned men across the nation). The court essentially determined that the trial judge had erred in allowing jurors who were morally opposed to the death penalty to be removed from the potential jury pool.[259] Speck's conviction was not overturned by the court, and he was taken back to the Peoria County Courthouse in November 1972 and given a sentence of 400 to 1,200 years in prison.

"As the sentence was pronounced, there was no visible reaction from Speck, who sat with his back to reporters" *The Chicago Tribune* reported. "However, when he rose to leave the courtroom, some observers saw a hint of a smile flash across his face."[260]

Confined to the Stateville Penitentiary in Crest Hills, Illinois, Speck refused all requests for reporter interviews until he agreed to talk with *Chicago Tribune* columnist Bob Greene. Speck made his first public confession of the killings in his interviews with Greene, but never again discussed the case publicly.[261]

In 1996, five years after he died on December 6, 1991, Speck showed up in clandestine sex tapes made inside the prison by the prisoners in 1988. In the tape, Speck is shown engaging in oral sex with other inmates, and appears to have altered his appearance to look like a female.[262]

Corazon Amurao went on to a long career in nursing in both the Philippines, and for the Georgetown University Medical Center, and the Veterans Administration Medical

Center, both in Washington, D. C. Married and a grandmother, she rarely talks publicly about the case but told one of her Chicago friends about that day long ago, “I think there was somebody up there who was hiding me from [Speck]. God was so nice.”[263]

The Bizarre Trial of Charlie and His Girls

LOS ANGELES COUNTY HALL OF JUSTICE

June 1970-January 1971—Los Angeles, California

As the $230 million renovation of the historic Los Angeles Hall of Justice was unveiled in October 2014, an interesting relic of the building's past was revealed as having survived the massive makeover.

"A single grim artifact has been preserved: the claustrophobic jail cell occupied by Charles Manson, Sirhan Sirhan and other celebrity defendants," veteran Associated Press trial writer Linda Deutsch wrote. "It's in the basement where the county coroner once performed autopsies on Marilyn Monroe and Sen. Robert F. Kennedy."[264]

The building, completed in 1925 as a mammoth piece of

downtown Los Angeles' "civic center" area, it has survived many challenges, but the 1994 Northridge earthquake (that reached 6.7 on the Richter scale) that rocked Los Angeles County was too much. The quake caused significant structural damage to the building, forcing the movement of dozens of courtrooms and hundreds of jail holding cells.

In its past, the Hall of Justice served as the backdrop for numerous television shows (such as "*Dragnet*") and films over the years. It also had hosted some of the nation's most noteworthy trials, including (at the time) the longest trial in US history.

From June 1970 to January 1971, the LA Hall of Justice housed the surreal and often troubling trial of cult leader and accused mass killer, Charles Manson and his followers. As Deutsch wrote, Manson's trial "drew a huge press corps. Members of his ragtag 'family' camped on the sidewalk giving interviews and threatening to set themselves on fire if their leader was convicted. One Manson follower, surrendered on the Hall of Justice steps surrounded by dozens of news crews. Another Manson acolyte, jailed on lesser charges, tied bed sheets together and escaped."[265]

Deutsch reported that during the trial, some of Manson's supporters suffered "LSD flashbacks" and were dragged out of the courtroom shouting. Members of the Manson family "worshiped him and compared him to Jesus." During the trial, Manson's followers "became a tourist attraction and were always available for media interviews."[266]

The trial was based on the bloody and brutal slayings of seven people over two days in Los Angeles. The first five murders occurred inside and on the lawn of an opulent Beverly Hills-area estate located at 10050 Cielo Drive. At the time, the home was rented by award-winning film director Roman Polanski and his actress wife, Sharon Tate.

Officially charged with the murders were Manson and three of his female followers: Patricia Krenwinkel, twenty-two years old; Susan Atkins, twenty-one; and Leslie Van Houten, twenty.

The five persons found dead at the Cielo Drive home on August 9, 1969, included: Tate, twenty-seven years old (eight months pregnant with Polanski's child); coffee heiress Abigail Folger, twenty-six; hair stylist Jay Sebring, thirty-seven; Polish filmmaker Wojceich Frykowski, thirty-seven; and Steven Parent, eighteen, a friend of the caretaker of the Benedict Canyon home where the murders occurred.

Killed the next night on August 10, 1969 were: Leon La Bianca, forty-four years old; and his wife, Rosemary, thirty-eight, owners of a small chain of southern California grocery stores. Pathologists determined all of the victims suffered a variety of wounds, from dozens of stab wounds, throttling of the neck and gunshot wounds.

At the Tate home murder scene, some of the victim's blood was used to write the word "pig" on a door. At the La Bianca scene, police found the word "death" and "death to pigs" also written in blood.

On the opening day of the trial, Manson, thirty-five years old, appeared with an X-cross scratched into the skin of his forehead, matching a bloody symbol left at the murder scenes. Defense attorneys for Manson explained the cross was carved by their client himself using a razor blade and reflected how he had continually referred to himself as "Jesus Christ."

"The three girls [on trial with Manson] were much more animated [than Manson] from the start of things," Green reported. "They sat close together, talked among themselves often, and seemed to joke with Manson during the breaks. They were huddled together like three young girls who had been sent to the principal's office."

In his opening argument against Manson and his co-defendants, Vincent T. Bugliosi, a deputy district attorney, said the evil of the "Manson Family" had been inspired by the Beatles song "Helter Skelter" in order to start "a black-white revolution." Bugliosi told jurors, Manson "believed the Beatles were speaking to him from across the ocean." The song lyrics, which included "helter skelter" and "rise" were among the words left behind at the murder scene.[267]

"The words meant the black man was rising up against the white establishment and murdering the entire white race," Bugliosi said. "The evidence will show that Charles Manson hated black people but also hated whites whom he called pigs."[268]

Prosecutors alleged the three women—Kernwinkel, Atkins and Van Houten, along with Charles "Tex" Watson, twenty-four years old—had killed the victims but had done so at the direction of Manson. Bugliosi called Manson "a killer who cleverly masqueraded behind a pose of a hippie . . . a megalomaniac who coupled his insatiable thirst for power with a desire for violent death."[269]

Theories on a motive for the crimes ranged from Manson's alleged desire to start a race war between black and white citizens in the United States to Manson's continued resentment over his stalled music career. Trial testimony would later reveal Manson had once auditioned for record producer Terry Melcher, the only son of famed Hollywood actress Doris Day, at the home on Cielo Drive where Polanski and Tate now lived. Melcher later testified he auditioned Manson, but did not find his talent worthy of pursuing.

The state's "star" witness was expected to be Linda Kasabian, a twenty-one-year-old former follower of Manson who revealed that she and others were "slavishly obedient" to Manson. Bugliosi described the mission of Manson and his followers as one of murder. "On this night [in August 1969], in this vast sprawling metropolis of over seven million people, no one was safe from Manson's lust for blood, death and murder."[270]

On the day Kasabian was called to testify, a group of Manson's other female followers sat eerily outside the Hall of Justice, hoping to see her and "stare her down" for her disloyalty to Manson. On the witness stand, Kasabian said she had joined "the family" in July 1969, just a month before the murders, and confirmed that she witnessed three of the seven murders. She had been granted immunity from prosecution for her testimony.

Kasabian said she joined the Manson "family" of about 20 members at the invitation of a friend named "Gypsy," who told her that Manson was "a beautiful man that we'd all been waiting for" and that Manson had sized her up physically and asked her questions about her interest in the group. "We lived together," she said, "as one family—as a mother, father, and children, only all as one, and Charlie was the head."[271]

During additional testimony, Kasabian denied she understood they were going to the Tate home to commit murder. "I thought we were going on a creepy-crawly mission, where you go into people's houses and take things that actually belong to you because everything belongs to everybody," she said.[272]

She said she witnessed the murders of everyone except Tate and Sebring, and even apologized to Frykowski as he was dying from as many as fifty-one stab wounds. Kasabian sobbed as "she told how her fear turned into horror as the grim tableau continued," the AP reported. "While she waited outside the Tate residence, she recalled hearing the screams of the victims, then seeing Miss Folger and Frykowski, both covered with blood, running from the front door."[273]

Her direct testimony was, "Katie [Krenwinkel] was chasing the woman in the white gown [Folger] with an upraised knife, and Tex [Charles Watson] caught the man [Frykowski] when he fell and began beating him on the head and stabbing him. They kept doing it and doing it. I don't have any words to describe it. It was unbelievably terrible and horrible."[274]

She also testified that Manson was present outside the palatial Tate-Polanski home and "told us to leave a sign. He said, 'You girls know what I mean, something witchy.'" The result was the words "helter skelter" scrawled in blood inside the home.[275]

Kasabian also described the La Bianca murders that came on August 10, 1969, the day after the five murders were discovered in Benedict Canyon. Kasabian said Manson directed his followers to drive around Los Angeles for hours at a time until he finally settled on entering the La Bianca home at 3301 Waverly Drive in the well-appointed Los Feliz neighborhood of Los Angeles.

Kasabian detailed the aftermath of the killings, but again placed the blame for the actual acts of murder upon other members of the family. She even testified that Krenwinkel had injured her hand while stabbing the victims "because the knife kept hitting bones."[276]

When the murders were done, Kasabian quoted "Tex" Watson, Manson's top lieutenant, as saying: "I am the devil here to the devil's work. He said that was what he had told the people [that he murdered]. And he said there was a lot of panic and it was really, really messy, and there were bodies all over the place, but that they were all dead."[277]

During her testimony, Manson briefly interrupted Kasabian by saying, "You're lying." Kasabian stared at Manson for a moment and replied, "It's not a lie, Charlie."[278] She later testified that she defied an order by Manson to kill a man who had been intimate with her.

It appeared the three young girls on trial with Manson were intent upon trying to intimidate Kasabian. They arrived in court the day of her testimony with "X" marks on their foreheads, similar to the one Manson sported. "Kasabian avoided the steady stares of the three women defendants as she sat on the witness stand during the at-bench conferences [of attorneys]," *The Los Angeles Times* reported.

Manson's interruption was not the only one—after issuing more than 50 objections to prosecution questions posed to Kasabian and an obscene gesture given in court—Judge Charles H. Older ordered two defense attorneys, Irvin A. Kanarek and Ronald Hughes held overnight in jail on a contempt of court charge. Eventually, two other attorneys were also charged with contempt before the bizarre trial was concluded, including Bugliosi who lost his cool during a court session in October.

Far from the courthouse, President Richard Nixon caused a short stir in the trial when he told reporters in Denver that he believed Manson was guilty of the murder charges. "Here is a man who was guilty, directly or indirectly, of eight murders without reason," Nixon said. "Here is a man, yet, who as far as the [news] coverage was concerned, appeared to be a rather glamorous figure to the young people whom he had brought into his operations."[279]

Upon returning to the White House, Nixon clarified that he did intend to say that Manson was guilty, and that the matter of guilt was to be determined by the jury. "The last thing I would do is prejudice the legal rights of any person, in any circumstances," Nixon said. "To set the record straight, I do not now and did not intend to speculate as to whether the Tate defendants are guilty, in fact, or not."[280]

Somehow, Manson himself obtained and briefly displayed in the courtroom a copy of *The Los Angeles Times* bearing a headline about Nixon's remarks—and a defense motion for a mistrial was angrily debated (and rejected) outside the company of the jury.

While the trial was underway, a "time bomb" exploded in a sixth-floor restroom of the building, opening a nine-by-eleven foot hole in a wall and bursting a water main, causing a cascading flood on lower floors. The bomb went off around 1 a.m. on September 6, 1970, and caused no injuries. At the time, investigators were unsure if the bombing was related to the ongoing Manson trial. It was later determined the bomb was the work of the Weather Underground (a radical political group) in protest of a journalist killed by police at a Vietnam War protest.[281]

As the trial wore on, on October 1, 1970, Manson and the three female defendants were ordered from the courtroom after disrupting proceedings and calling Judge Older "a woman." At first Older ordered Manson and the women removed to an adjoining room of the courtroom where they could hear the audio proceedings over a small speaker. He later decided to dismiss court for the day.

Manson's interruption began as his defense attorney tried to cross-examine a state witness. "Oh, the old gray mare she ain't what she used to be," Manson began singing in a high-pitched voice. "The old gray mare she ain't what she used to be. She's a judge now."[282]

As Judge Older attempted to silence Manson, he told the judge, "You don't have authority. You are a woman."[283]

"Mr. Manson, I will have to remove you from the courtroom if you don't stop it," Older warned.[284]

Manson replied that the judge should "stop what *you're* doing" and added, "You have ordered me to stop living. You won't let my lawyer visit me. You won't let me have any mail. I can't get any action in the attorney room. My lawyer can't even come into the lockup. I am allowed to talk to him at the bench for five minutes a day. How am I supposed to prove a case and prove anything to these people?"[285]

With that Older ordered Manson from the room, and he left without incident. Allowed to return 35 minutes later, Manson again interrupted proceedings by proclaiming, "I would like everyone to know I'm not represented in this trial. I do not have a lawyer. I'm not allowed to speak for myself."[286]

When Judge Older told bailiffs to remove Manson from the courtroom a second time, the female defendants began chanting and singing a song aimed at the judge: "You are just a woman. You are just a woman. That is all." The women ridiculed the judge's tie as they "strutted from the courtroom" led by sheriff's deputies.[287]

The raucous nature of the proceedings continued days later on October 5, 1970 when Manson attempted to jump over the defense table and attack Judge Older: "Charles Manson leaped over a counsel table in an attempt to attack [the judge] . . . startling jurors in the Tate-La Bianco murder trial. But, as Manson sprang with a pencil in his hand, Sheriff's Deputy William Murray was after him. The deputy, a strapping six feet, two inches, landed on Manson's back, driving the bearded five-foot, five-inch defendant to the floor. Two other deputies joined Murray in a brief struggle with Manson in front of the bench."[288]

Unmoved was Judge Older, who did not flinch during the incident, reporters noted. As he was scurried from the courtroom, Manson yelled at Judge Older, "In the name of Christian justice, someone should cut off your head."[289]

With that, Manson's codefendants, called "Charlie's girls" by reporters, began to chant: "Na ho-ram, ky-o, nam-na, ho-ram, ky-o."[290]

Judge Older said to the women, "I order you to stop or your will be removed." Atkins, Krenwinkel and Van Houten were unmoved and clearly still took their cues from Manson.

Atkins said, "Mr. Older, you are not my judge. You are not my God. You may be these people's God [turning toward the spectator section of the courtroom], but you're not mine."[291]

Krenwinkel followed suit, announcing, "I will not accept your justice. I judge myself—you judge yourself. I cannot accept this courtroom."[292]

Van Houten added, "Your law will lead you to self-destruction."[293]

With that, all three women were removed from the courtroom.

Just before he attempted to attack the jurist, Manson questioned Judge Older in a sarcastic tone: "Are you going to use this courtroom to kill me? Do you want me dead?"[294]

Manson then threatened the judge, "The minute I see you're going to kill me, you know what I'm going to do?"

Exasperated, Judge Older replied, "What are you going to do?"

Manson replied, "You know, you have studied your book. You know who you are talking to. . . . Order me to be quiet while you kill me with your courtroom? Does that make sense? Am I supposed to lay here and just let you kill me? I am a human being. I am going to fight for my life, one way or another. You should let me do it with words."[295]

Not surprisingly, defense attorneys argued that the courtroom outbursts occurring in front of the jury supported the need to declare a mistrial. Judge Older was having none of it, dismissing repeated dismissal motions by defense counsel. In total, the four defendants were kept in an adjoining room for more than two weeks because of their outbursts in court.

In total, prosecutors called 80 witnesses over ninety-eight days of court, and entered 300 exhibits, including a large array of photographs depicting the two grisly murder scenes in the case.

Defense attorneys struggled for a strategy to defend their clients, not only because their clients were at best described as "eccentric" but also uncooperative. The list of potential defense witnesses included Mama Cass Eliott and John Phillips, both former members of the singing group the Mamas and the Papas (though neither were ever called as witnesses—Manson being the only defense witness who ever testified at trial).

As the defense case began, Atkins joined Manson in her insistence that she represent herself in the case. The judge refused their request, and Atkins's attorney refused to cooperate in asking her more than sixty questions she wrote for him to ask her under oath. At one point, the three women were briefly subdued by sheriff's deputies when they attempted to approach the bench to join a conference between the judge and the attorneys in the case.

The defense attorneys for the three women quickly rested their cases without calling the women (or anyone else) to testify. The women were reportedly ready to confess on the stand that they had conducted the murders for which they were accused.

Manson took the stand himself on November 20, 1970, testifying for more than an hour about his theories about the case against him, the Vietnam War, LSD, and President Nixon. Referring to Judge Older as "God," Manson said, "I never went to school, so I never growed up in the respect to learn, to read and write too good, so I have stayed in jail and I have stayed stupid, and I have stayed a child while I have watched your world grow up and then I look at the things that you do and I don't understand."[296]

Manson referred to "the children" of the nation and said, "These children that come at you with knives, they are your children. You taught them. I didn't teach them. I just tried to help them stand up. Most of the people at the ranch that you call the 'family' were just people that you did not want, people that were alongside the road, that their parents had kicked them out or they did not want to go to juvenile hall. So I did the best I could and I took them up to my garbage dump. I told them this: That in love there is no wrong."[297]

As he cast himself as a victim of society, Manson said, "I have done my best to get along in your world now you want to kill me. I have killed no one and I have ordered no one to be killed. I may have implied that I may have been Jesus Christ. But I haven't decided yet what I am and who I am."[298]

The trial took another odd turn later in November 1970 when Van Houten's attorney, Ronald Hughes, went missing during a long court recess. He failed to show for court and Judge Older eventually appointed a different attorney to finish the trial on Van Houten's behalf. The decomposed body of Hughes was found months later, ironically the same day Manson and the three women were sentenced to death for the murders.

Investigators were never able to determine the cause of Hughes' death—some believing he was drown in a flash flood while camping, while at least one Manson family member said Hughes was killed in retribution by supporters of Manson and Van Houten.

On March 29, 1971, Manson family members again called attention to themselves outside the courtroom. On a sidewalk outside the Hall of Justice, four female members of "the family" sat in a circle with their shaved heads and sang songs. Dubbed by reporters, "the girls on the corner," the women, Cathy Gillies, Kitty Lutesinger, Sandy Good, and Brenda McCann, said they were keeping a vigil for their leader, Manson.

The next day Mason, Atkins, Krenwinkel and Van Houten were sentenced to death but were not present to hear the sentence as they had been removed from the courtroom again after causing a disruption. Manson remained in prison in California until his death on November 19, 2017 at the age of eighty-three. Watson, Krenwinkel, and Van Houten remain incarcerated. Atkins died of brain cancer in prison on September 24, 2009 at the age of sixty-one.

An Obscene Display of Street Justice

GWINNETT COUNTY COURTHOUSE

March 6, 1978—Lawrenceville, Georgia

Photo Courtesy of Joanne Speirs Littlefield

Gene Reeves Jr. was a hard-working, but obscure county seat lawyer in small-town Georgia in 1978 until one day the phone rang. Out of the blue came a client he never counted on—Larry Flynt—king of the *Hustler* magazine conglomerate built on edgy pornography, and biting, unforgiving political satire.

Flynt had run afoul of authorities in Gwinnett County, a red clay suburban community thirty miles northeast of Atlanta. His *Hustler* magazine and its open, unflinching portrayal of almost every conceivable aspect of human sexuality was more than most locals could abide.

Reeves was enlisted by Flynt's other high-priced counsel to help fight the charges in Georgia. Accepting the provocative Flynt as a client had risks, but "As far as career-wise, it probably helped me, because at least people knew who I was. A lot of people figured, 'Well, Flynt hired him—I'll hire him,' you know," Reeves said.[299]

The trial at Lawrenceville, Georgia was Flynt's second go-round on obscenity charges. In 1976, a jury in his hometown of Cincinnati, Ohio had found him guilty of engaging in organized crime and pandering obscenity. A sentence of seven to twenty-five years was imposed, along with an $11,000 fine, but Flynt remained free on an appeal bond at the time of the Georgia trial.

In Georgia, state prosecutors, led by Solicitor Gary Davis, said that a July 1976 issue of *Hustler* magazine—which Flynt had dubbed his "Super Bicentennial Issue"—violated Georgia's obscenity laws against "the sale of material appealing to prurient, morbid or shameful interest in nudity, sex and excretion."[300] The magazine's cover, featuring a close-up shot of a woman's American flag bikini bottom revealing a scruff of pubic hair, was dubbed one of the most controversial ever (and was later mimicked by the Black Crowes for their 1994 "Amorica" album).[301]

The trial against Flynt opened at the old Gwinnett County Courthouse in Lawrenceville on March 3, 1978 but seemed to draw more interest from regional and national media than from any locals—the spectator section of the courtroom was mostly empty except for reporters.

On Friday, March 6, 1978, a smug thirty-five-year-old Flynt took the stand to testify on his own behalf, describing *Hustler* magazine as "one big put-on" and that "We are as much a humor magazine dealing with satire as we are a sexual magazine."[302] Flynt disclosed in his testimony that

Hustler magazine reached as many as fifty million readers each month.

While *Hustler* was a success, Flynt also said he had been bankrupt twice before he was thirty-years-old before when he owned chain of his *Hustler* stripper clubs in Cincinnati, Dayton, Columbus, Cleveland, and Akron, Ohio. The magazine, of the same name, grew out of the club's success. His first stripper club opened in Akron, Ohio in 1967 and the magazine grew out of the club's four-page newsletter.[303]

Flynt acknowledged that some of the content of *Hustler* magazine offended some of his own morals, especially since his Christian conversion. He clarified that some items in the magazine could be "wrong" but not "illegal." He explained: "I feel drinking is wrong, but it's not illegal."[304]

As the morning session drew to a close, Flynt walked across the street from the courthouse to the V & J Cafeteria on Perry Street—as he reportedly did every day—with reporters and defense attorneys in tow. His lunch finished, Flynt walked back to the west entrance of the courthouse alongside his local attorney, Reeves. Lead attorney Harold P. Fahringer was a few steps ahead of the two men.

Just then, two loud cracks rang out, coming from an unknown direction.

Neil Shister, a reporter for the Flynt-owned *Atlanta Gazette*, who witnessed the shooting said, "I was about twenty feet behind him. I heard a loud report and looked to see if a car had backfired. I immediately smelled gunpowder. Larry had fallen down and was clutching his side."[305]

"The attempted assassination was clouded in confusion," United Press International reported. "A witness said Reeves fell on his back by a telephone pole and Flynt staggered to the steps of a [nearby] store, where he fell face down."[306]

Conflicting witness reports emerged—some claiming a man had walked up to the two men and fired a gun, while others were certain a black and silver car had sped by with a shooter hitting the men from the car. In the end, neither of those accounts were factual.

Investigation showed Flynt and Reeves were cut down by a .44 caliber Marlin rifle—a rifle normally used to hunt large game. The shots had been fired from the second floor of a former hotel on Perry Street.

Gwinnett County Police issued a statement confirming that two shots were fired at the men, one striking Flynt in the stomach. The second shot struck Reeves in the arm and traveled through to his stomach.[307]

Confusion set in as the limitations of small-town Georgia came to the fore—Lawrenceville having just one ambulance available. No one was sure which of the two mortally wounded men should be transported first. In the end, both were loaded in the same ambulance and rushed to Button Gwinnett Hospital in Lawrenceville.

Flynt underwent four hours of surgery for the massive bullet wounds to his abdomen, including removal of a large portion of his intestine. Reeves's injuries were less severe, although he was hospitalized for more than a month afterward.

Back at the courthouse, blood stained the sidewalk along Perry Street and the Gwinnett County Prosecutor's Office confirmed they had received a phone call about twenty minutes after the shooting. The caller told a clerk who answered the phone: "You won't have to worry about Larry Flynt anymore. Jesus has taken a hand in it."[308]

Bullet casings were removed from a second floor room of the abandoned hotel on Perry Street, opposite the west face of the courthouse.

"Police cordoned off the two-story [hotel] structure, in which several window panes are broken," the Associated Press reported. "Reporters said they saw technicians taking plaster casts—used in identifying footprints or tire tracks—from behind the building in an alleyway."[309]

Flynt's lead attorney Fahringer was among the first to reach Flynt as he lay bleeding on the sidewalk after he was struck down by bullets. He accompanied Flynt in an ambulance to the hospital and said, "He tried to say something but I couldn't make it out."[310]

"I think this is very sad, a commentary on our society," Fahringer said. "We are living in a neurotic civilization. Flynt, who was on trial for simply publishing a magazine, is shot."[311]

Flynt would later describe the courthouse attack—as expected—in graphic detail in his 1996 memoir, *"An Unseemly Man."* After being shot, he recalled:

> I looked down and saw that my intestines were spilling out of my body. The first shot had hit at an odd angle and nearly rippled the front of my stomach off. I couldn't tell where the second shot had gone. As my knees buckled and I began to lose consciousness, the first thought that went through my mind was, 'Shit! I'm not going to finish the trial today!' It was inconceivable to me that I might die.[312]

Reeves, the small-town Georgia attorney enlisted to help in Flynt's defense, recalled the day many years later in an interview for *Atlanta* magazine. Reeves remembered:

> It was a nice, pretty day. It was mild. We had on suits with coats but no overcoats or anything like that. . . . [Flynt] and I were walking together, and when the shooting

> occurred, they didn't hit me, they hit him. I think there were two shots. One of them hit him in the spine; the other one was a flesh wound that went through him and into my arm, stomach, and pancreas. But you got to realize it was a .44 magnum, which is sort of an elephant gun.[313]

Reeves said "it looked like someone picked [Flynt] up and threw him about four or five feet, as he took the impact of the bullet. He was on the ground, and I recall I got up and tried to see how he was. About that time, I passed out."[314]

Flynt's twenty-four-year-old wife Althea, accompanied by evangelist Ruth Carter Stapleton (the sister of President Jimmy Carter), flew to Georgia to be at his bedside.

Prior to the trial at Lawrenceville, Flynt had made national headlines after proclaiming that he had become a "born again" Christian through the evangelism of Stapleton, the younger sister of President Carter. Flynt had vowed to make changes to *Hustler* magazine to reflect his new views. In addition, he had attempted to expand his publishing empire in a bold manner, purchasing newspapers in Atlanta, Los Angeles, and in the President's home town, tiny Plains, Georgia.

Although he had officially stepped down as publisher of *Hustler*, he gave one example of a change at *Hustler*, transforming a regular cartoon character from "Chester the Molester" to "Chester the Protector."[315]

"We will try to do what God would approve of in our stories and pictures," Flynt assured reporters outside the Lawrenceville courthouse in the days before he was shot. "You will still see a tremendous amount of explicit sex in *Hustler*; no more explicit than what can be found in the Bible. And we will be sure to provide these references for our stories and pictorial features."[316]

Stapleton spoke to reporters outside the hospital, saying she spoke briefly to Flynt in the intensive care unit where he told her, "I'm going to make it" but had not been able to speak long enough to give police much of a statement.[317]

"Larry is a baby Christian," Stapleton said, asking fellow Christians to pray for his recovery. "I believe in miracles. I just thank God that he's alive," she added.[318]

For the first time, Stapleton also revealed she had been prepared to come to Georgia to testify on behalf of Flynt because of his religious conversion. She said Flynt had counseled her not to do so—"he was afraid it might hurt my ministry, it might hurt my family, it might hurt [President] Jimmy [Carter]. I told him I didn't think it would be that bad, but he insisted" she not participate in the trial.[319]

After surviving the assassination attempt but suffering painful and permanent paralysis below the waist, Flynt personally authorized the infamous June 1978 *Hustler* cover that depicted a nude woman's body being fed into a meat grinder. It was "accompanied by the promise that I would no longer treat women like a 'piece of meat.' It was my flat-footed attempt at apology [but] no one seemed to understand."[320]

Flynt said the magazine was intended to be "outrageous," and as *The New York Times* reported, "Mr. Flynt's magazine is widely regarded as far more distasteful than sexual, sometimes featuring scatological material and nude photographs of pregnant women and sixty-year-old women."[321]

Flynt clarified that "Even though I had been born again, my stance on the First Amendment had not changed. I decided to fight the [Georgia] indictment vigorously" and confirmed Stapleton's claim that he refused her offers to help.[322]

With *Hustler*, Flynt said his dream was to create "a sex magazine free of pretense and full of fantasy, fiction, satire and biting humor. I wanted to offend everyone on an equal-opportunity basis. I decided to run cartoons lampooning blacks, whites, Jews, Christians, rich and poor."[323]

While in Georgia for the obscenity trial and before he

was shot, Flynt had been his regular flamboyant self, eating lunch with reporters near the courthouse, and engaging a sidewalk evangelist outside the courthouse who condemned his magazine and his faith. Flynt had told the minster just days before he was shot, "I'm at peace with myself. I don't have any fear," *The New York Times* reported.[324]

Flynt walked about quiet downtown Lawrenceville without body guards—"totally accessible" as one reporter put it. His attorney, Fahringer said, "We knew when we came into this county that it was conservative and there would be some hostility toward us. But I never thought there would be anything as vicious as this."[325]

As the investigation dragged on, a disagreement opened between Flynt (and his family) and Gwinnett County officials about who may be responsible for the attempted assassination. "Some agents of the government were involved," Larry Flynt told one reporter.[326]

His wife Althea and his out-spoken brother Jimmy, were more specific in their theory, offering that either the Federal Bureau of Investigation or the Central Intelligence Agency were involved in the shooting. They based their theory on the fact that Flynt had used his publications to offer rewards for information regarding the assassinations of President John F. Kennedy and the Rev. Martin Luther King, Jr.

Gwinnett County officials were direct about their doubt: "We are not investigating the CIA or the FBI," said Bryant Huff, the Gwinnett County District Attorney at the time of the shooting.[327]

"The truth is the investigation is concentrating on the actual trigger people," Huff said. "Once the trigger people are determined, then I think the behind-the-scene people, so to speak, will be most evident."[328]

Huff said his office had ruled out any members of the Flynt family in the shooting and members of the Georgia Ku Klux Klan, but had not eliminated the idea that a rival in the porn business, or even organized crime figures could be responsible.

Disgruntled employees of Flynt's *Hustler* empire were not in the clear, however, Huff said, noting that Flynt had fired about twenty percent of his staff in recent months—including his brother Jimmy—if they did not accept Flynt's religious conversion.

Flynt confirmed the tension that had exploded within his company, telling a reporter that "*Hustler* is a one-man show. Anytime I get people thinking they are me, they have got to go out the door. As far as I am concerned, anyone who works for me is going to accept my conversion. And it's my company. If I want to spend the money, that's the way it's going to be."[329]

Althea Flynt (who later died in a drowning accident in her home in 1997) was famously quoted at the time as saying that "When Jesus walked into Larry's life, twenty-five million dollars walked out the door." Regarding the shooting, Mrs. Flynt said in 1978 that she did not trust the police who were investigating the case. She asserted, "all policemen are pigs" and "I am not sure I can depend on them."[330]

Huff scoffed at the claims by the Flynt's about who might be involved—"Larry Flynt does not have any idea who shot him or the reasons why he was shot."[331]

While a handful of initial arrests of suspects in Georgia and Virginia were reported related to the case, no one faced formal charges for shooting Flynt and Reeves until a Gwinnett County grand jury indicted thirty-four-year-old Joseph Paul Franklin on June 12, 1984.

Franklin, a notorious racist and sniper, was already serving a federal sentence for a racially-motivated murder, and was under either under investigation or indictment in several other states at the time. He ultimately was linked to as many as twenty murders, six aggravated assaults, sixteen bank robberies, and two bombings.

In 1997, Franklin told Kim Bell, a reporter for *The St.*

Louis Post-Dispatch, that he decided upon trying to kill Flynt when he first saw a *Hustler* magazine on a newsstand. The magazine in question, the December 1975 issue, included sexually explicit photos of an interracial couple titled "Butch: A Black Stud and His Georgia Peach."

"I just saw blood," Franklin said about viewing the pictures.[332]

"I threw the magazine down and I thought, 'I'm gonna kill that guy.'"[333]

Franklin said that sex between black and white people angered him and could lead to physical deformities, such as flabby skin.[334] In 2013, Franklin told CNN that the *Hustler* pictures "made me sick. I think whites marry with whites, blacks with blacks, Indians with Indians, Orientals with Orientals."[335]

Franklin implicated himself in the case by detailing the building where the shots came from—and confirmed he had been following Flynt both in Ohio and Georgia in the days before the shooting.

"He described the escape route, the vehicle he used, where he drove, and we were able to corroborate at least points of it," said Gwinnett County District Attorney Danny Porter.[336]

"Franklin has obliquely admitted shooting Flynt in several confessions to other crimes," Porter said. Franklin never faced trial for the Lawrenceville courthouse shooting—the indictment was dropped after the State of Missouri executed Franklin on November 20, 2013.[337]

Porter explained that his office reviewed the entire case before indicting Franklin, noting: "If you go over and look at where the shooting occurred, you can pretty much figure out how he got away. . . . He fired the shots, and then he just scooted out the back door and across that empty parking lot—and was gone. He told [investigators] that he had a car parked there and that he just drove off."[338]

Gacy's Gruesome Road to Justice

COOK COUNTY CRIMINAL COURTS BUILDING

February-March 1980—Chicago, Illinois

Photo courtesy of Ann Fisher

The thirty-three murders of young men John Wayne Gacy carried out were some of the most gruesome crimes in the history of Illinois. That fact notwithstanding, public interest and curiosity about his 1980 trial at the well-worn Cook County Criminal Courts Building in Chicago made certain courtroom seats would be coveted.

"There was a long line outside of Judge Louis Garippo's courtroom," on opening day, *Chicago Tribune* columnist Anne Keegan wrote. "It has been years since the high-ceilinged, marble Criminal Courts Building at 26th Street and California Avenue has held such a crowd. Not since the days of pretrial hearings for Richard Speck and the sensational trials of cigar-chomping Mafiosi."[339]

Gacy, who was thirty-seven-years-old as his trial opened, had been arrested just before Christmas on December 22, 1978, after offering (and later withdrawing) a confession that he had lured more than two-dozen young men to his home, and killed them.

Gacy's non-descript ranch-style home, located at 8213 Summerdale Avenue in Norwood Township (about fifteen miles northwest of the downtown Chicago loop), hid a horrible secret. In the crawl space beneath the home, the remains of twenty-nine men were partially buried and rotting. Another three men's bodies were found under a concrete slab in the driveway and garage behind the home.

His last victim was dumped off a bridge into the Des Plaines River as Gacy ran out of room to bury another victim.

Eventually, investigators dismantled the home Gacy had bought more than a decade earlier with financial help from family members who hoped he was turning the corner on his troubled past. Married and the adoptive father of two daughters, Gacy's ultimately futile attempts at respectability would struggle for pre-eminence in his life.

There was an evil, dark side of Gacy the son, husband, father, building contractor, community volunteer and good citizen. When alone, Gacy filled his hours with cruising Chicago streets looking for vulnerable and often disconnected young men to abduct, rape and murder.

The last young man he lured to his death, fifteen-year-old Robert Piest, had fallen for one of Gacy's regular tricks. Working part-time at a local pharmacy, Piest was excited about the bigger salary Gacy promised the attractive boy, to come to work for PDM Contracting. Named by Gacy for its Painting, Decorating and Maintenance, the company was a frequent front to attract young victims.

Unlike many of the other men who became victims of Gacy, the family of Piest was demanding of local police in trying to find their loved one. When Piest went missing family members knew something was wrong. Detectives and family members quickly surfaced the name of Gacy as the person who made an appointment with the high schooler on the day he went missing.

Detained for questioning on December 21, 1978, Gacy implicated himself in the Piest case and others, and was arrested the next day. Arraigned on 33 counts of murder, Gacy was led past a sparsely decorated Christmas tree in a corridor of a satellite courthouse in Des Plaines for a preliminary hearing, looking bloated and disheveled.

Months of investigations revealed the scope of the case, with new stories emerging almost every day of more bodies found under Gacy's home. At the same time, families and friends of missing men who had searched for them in vain turned over dental records to assist in identifying the remains.

For the trial, attorneys for both sides agreed that while the trial would be conducted in Cook County, jurors would be selected from Winnebago County. A horde of reporters and photographers camped outside the Winnebago County Public Safety Building in Rockford, Illinois, about nintey miles west of Chicago, to catch a glimpse of Gacy.

"Extraordinary security measures" were in place to transfer Gacy from the isolation cells of the Cook County Jail to isolation cells in the Winnebago County Jail. "Most of the reporters and photographers who had been waiting for hours in the winter cold for a glimpse of Gacy had gone home when the unmarked station wagon carrying him screeched around a corner and sped into a garage," *The Chicago Tribune* reported. "A Cook County sheriff's deputy holding a shotgun jumped from his car and kept a photographer at bay as Gacy passed by."[340]

On Monday morning, January 28, 1980 jury selection got underway in the Winnebago County Courthouse and Gacy "appeared relaxed and sometimes jovial" during the proceedings. Described as "clean-shaven and much thinner than when he was arrested" Gacy wore a gray tweed suit. "Some spectators who had not seem him before mistook him at first for one of the lawyers," wrote *Chicago Tribune* reporter Jane Fritsch.[341]

Potential jurors were questioned at length about their views regarding the death penalty, homosexuality and insanity defenses. "Throughout the day, Gacy took notes, read legal papers, chatted with his attorneys, and turned in his swivel chair to scan the faces in the courtroom," Fritsch wrote. "He seemed particularly fascinated by a female sketch artist in the front row."[342]

Chicago Tribune columnist Keegan shared that members of the public who gathered at the courts building appeared impatient and anxious about getting a seat to get a glimpse "of the man who has been accused of murdering more human beings than anyone else in this country's history. Many in the crowd just wanted to get a look at him."[343]

Judge Garippo's courtroom had the only working clock in the building, reporters noted, repairs having been made before the start of the trial. Other upgrades were new carpeting for the jury box and a small chain separating the spectator section from the defendant and lawyers at the front.

Gacy, reporters again noting that he had lost weight from the time of his arrest having consumed an all-jail diet for thirteen months, was described in news accounts as a "suburban contractor, precinct captain, and occasional jolly clown."[344]

Although the remains of thirty-three men had been unearthed in the crawl space beneath Gacy's home, only twenty-two of them had been identified by the time of the trial. Despite that, state attorneys had the jawbones of thirty-three separate victims stored out of view in a conference room on an upper floor of the court building.

The families of only two of the identified victims, however, appeared for the trial. They were required to wait in line for courtroom seats alongside the curious onlookers.

Harold and Elizabeth Piest, grieved parents of Robert Piest (the last of Gacy's victims) were there as they had been for all pre-trial hearings. The other parent present, Lola Woods, was the mother of William Kindred who was reported missing in February 1978.

Mrs. Woods, the mother of ten children, told reporters, "I just felt I should come. I'm going to try to come here every day. I want to watch this whole thing. I want to see what they're going to do to this man. I'd like to see him killed like my boy was killed."[345]

Gacy seemed to take the actual trial more seriously than the pre-trial proceedings in Rockford. He did not smile and wave to audience members as he entered the Chicago courtroom, and instead kept his gaze fixed on the judge.

Opening arguments by both sides in the case were as sensational and painful as expected.

Assistant State's Attorney Robert Egan began:

> I want you to picture, if you will, a young boy, fifteen years old, a sophomore in high school, a gymnast, and in the evenings, he worked in a pharmacy. He was working [at the pharmacy] on the night of December 11, 1978. He was working there, stocking shelves and going about his usual duties. And there was someone else there, ladies and gentlemen. That somebody else was a contractor. . . . [someone] Robert Piest had never met before.[346]

Egan explained that the contractor, Gacy, talked to an excited Robert about a possible summer job that would pay more than the pharmacy job. Piest had agreed to go to Gacy's home to learn more about the job, and it was there Gacy employed his deadly "trick" of demonstrating handcuffs in an alleged "magic trick."

Explaining that Gacy had handcuffed Piest as a set-up for the "trick," there were no plans to remove the handcuffs. Instead, sexual acts were forced upon the young man, who was then strangled to death with a piece of knotted rope.

Gacy "twisted [the rope] and then he twisted it again, and he held it there, and it did just what a tourniquet would do. It broke the blood flow to the brain. No more air went into the lungs; Piest convulsed and was dead in seconds."[347]

As Egan described Robert's last moments of life, his twenty-two-year-old sister Kerry gripped her mother's hand as both women quietly wept.

Egan noted, however, that as disturbing as the details of the young man's death were, "That in itself is not the horrible part of the story. The horrible part is that this was the last of thirty-three young men, people with their lives ahead of them; that John Gacy strangled, killed, and buried."[348]

Egan went on to describe "Gacy's graveyard," as he termed it, found in the crawlspace that was only 30 inches deep underneath his home. He said Gacy "killed people like he was swatting flies" and conducted his evil in a "planned, mechanical, and premeditated manner."[349]

In statements given to detectives, Egan said Gacy had provided an excuse that he had to kill the young men either because they demanded more money for a sexual tryst, or threatened to expose his sexual advances upon them.

Gacy also admitted that one victim, Gregory Godzik, seventeen years old, had actually dug his own grave under the guise of creating a trench for a drain pipe in the crawl space—a hole in which Gacy later placed Godzik's lifeless body in in December 1976.

Egan acknowledged to jurors that some of the victims were male prostitutes who had gone with Gacy willingly, while others were sexually assaulted against their will once the handcuff "trick" was enacted.

Robert Motta, one of Gacy's defense attorneys, told jurors that sometimes a calm and engaging man, his client suffered from "an unconscious and uncontrollable mental illness" and as a result, could not be held responsible for his acts under Illinois law.

Motta said Gacy's crimes occurred "over and over and over again" because of a "profound and incredible obsession" and added:

> He sleeps with corpses. He lived in a house with bodies under it for years. He was incapable of forming an intent because of a profound mental disease. . . . His intelligence and thought processes were helpless against a consuming mental disease. . . . He knew something was happening and he couldn't help it. . . . He's dangerously and incomprehensively ill.[350]

Spectators jamming the courtroom for the trial were exposed to painful testimony from a series of eight mothers and one father who told of the last time they saw their sons alive. Several provided information that their sons knew Gacy, while others identified rings or other personal items found in Gacy's home.

One mother, Bessie Stapleton, hit her head on the witness stand as she cried out and wept when shown a picture of her son. "God, why!?" she called out from her sobs. Jurors were led out of the courtroom as ambulance personnel were summoned to treat Mrs. Stapleton for a small bump on her head.[351]

The Chicago Tribune noted that "paramedics stood by just outside the courtroom as witness after witness broke into tears," one of the mothers pleading with the judge: "Please ask Mr. Gacy to stop staring at me."[352]

Elizabeth Piest, the mother of the last victim, described the events of December 11, 1978, the last time she saw her son. She remembered the evening well because it was her birthday and her son was expected home to help celebrate it after his scheduled meeting at Gacy's home.

Her son, she said, was a sophomore and honor student at Maine West High School and was just two merit badges away from earning Eagle Scout status. Ironically, one of his last merit badge projects was to clean-up a river bank along the Des Plaines River, the same waterway where his body was dumped by Gacy.

Employed by the Nisson Pharmacy in Des Plaines, Mrs. Piest said Robert was saving up to buy a car. She had planned to give him a ride home that evening, but she said he instead wanted to go with Gacy to talk about a better paying summer job.

"He went outside [the pharmacy] and never came back," she said after waiting for him to return for twenty minutes. "I said something is wrong, we can't find Rob."[353]

The Piest family spent the rest of the evening searching for Robert rather than observing the birthday, which was their family tradition. Their efforts were in vain, along with printed up "missing person" fliers she and family members plastered all over the Des Plaines area.

Perhaps trying to access some of the sympathy the parade of victim's mothers likely drew from jurors, defense attorneys took their own turn and called Gacy's aged seventy-two-year-old mother. Marion Gacy, who walked slowly with the help of a walker, declared her son as "good hearted" and "loving."[354]

Accompanied by Gacy's only sibling, Karen Gacy Kuzma, the elderly woman had come to Chicago from her home in Little Rock, Arkansas. Kuzma also testified, saying her brother possessed "a sweet and generous character." Asked if she could conceive of her brother hurting anyone, Kuzma proclaimed, "No way, the brother that I knew was always sweet, loving, understanding, generous."[355]

"I love my son," Mrs. Gacy said. "I still don't believe any of it. I can't believe it. I can't believe he'd do any of it. Not my son. I'd just like to erase everything."[356]

As she began to weep, a short recess was called, allowing John Wayne Gacy to offer his mother a brief embrace as he was led from the courtroom. His mother's testimony prompted the only open emotion Gacy had displayed in the trial.

Testifying for more than eleven hours, Mrs. Gacy provided details of her son's life from the time he was born until he was arrested in 1978 and charged with the deaths of 33 men. She testified that he was a "sickly boy" and was frequently treated by doctors for blackouts, or possible epilepsy.

Mrs. Gacy confirmed that one doctor who examined her son as a teenager recommended that he receive psychiatric care. "John pleaded with me, 'Mom, don't send me to the psychiatric ward. I'll be good. So I went and signed him out, which I probably shouldn't have done."[357]

She also detailed a difficult relationship Gacy had with a domineering and sometimes violent and alcoholic father. She said her husband "seemed to be after John all the time. He always called him stupid."[358]

The father-son relationship was made worse, Mrs. Gacy testified, after her son was arrested and convicted in 1968 in Waterloo, Iowa on a sodomy charge involving the son of a prominent local citizen. Married and the father of two children,

Gacy's wife left him as he entered prison and his father died in 1969 while he was behind bars.

Beyond endearing sympathy from jurors, Mrs. Gacy's role set up defense efforts to link the sickening relationship between Gacy and his father as the basis for his mental problems. "Some of the psychiatrists [employed by the defense] view Gacy's homosexual relationships, which often included forms of bondage, as Gacy's reaction to his authoritarian father and as an attempt to put himself in the dominating role," *TheTribune's* Jane Fritsch wrote.[359]

Defense attorneys also called the only two men known to have escaped Gacy's advances. Jeffrey Rignall, who was twenty-six-years-old when he met Gacy on a Chicago street, said he went with him with the promise of a car ride and a marijuana cigarette.

Rignall said that Gacy used chloroform on him once he was inside Gacy's car, and was taken to the Norwood home where he was sexually molested. Rignall, who was highly agitated and at one pointed became nauseated while he testified, said he awoke the next morning partially clothed on a street in Lincoln Park, Illinois.

Rignall said Chicago Police refused to help him once they learned he was gay, and assumed that the incident was just a disagreement between two homosexuals.[360]

The defense also called Michael Reid, a young man who lived briefly with Gacy in 1971, and exchanged sexual acts for money and rent. He said he moved out after one sexual encounter became violent and Gacy struck him on the head with a hammer.[361]

Gacy apparently grew impatient with the proceedings, and outside of the counsel of his defense attorneys wrote two letters to Judge Garippo asking that his trial be stopped, and his attorneys fired. In his letters, Gacy expressed frustration that the motion for a dismissal was not granted, claiming the state's only evidence was that he owned the house where the bodies were found.

Garippo conducted a hearing on Gacy's letters, outside of the presence of the jury, on March 7, 1980. Gacy told the judge, "I would like to know myself if I committed the crimes," saying that he had undergone more than 300 hours of examinations by psychiatrists for the state and his defense.[362]

He told the judge that his statements were misconstrued by the news media: "Half the time, I leave the courtroom not knowing who I am. I believe that I've been tried, convicted and sentenced in the news media already. Nowhere in this land could I get a fair trial."[363]

Advised again that jurors would not reading news media accounts of the alleged crimes, and were to base their decision on courtroom testimony only, Gacy seemed to sense that the judge was not inclined to end the trial. Gacy sat down and said, "I did not commit the crimes."[364]

The judge also reminded Gacy that he still had the option to take the stand and testify on his own behalf, but Gacy did not reply (and never did testify).

"Based on my own observation of the defendant in the courtroom, based on his demeanor, I will enter a finding of fitness," Garippo said, and ordered the trial to go forward.[365]

Final arguments were heard on March 11 and 12, 1980 and after only two hours of deliberation, the jury convicted Gacy on all thirty-three counts of murder. Days later they also ordered a sentence of death for the killer.

Gacy was executed via lethal injection on May 11, 1994.

Seeking Justice for Matthew Shepard

ALBANY COUNTY COURTHOUSE
April, October-November 1999—Laramie, Wyoming

Between the compact University of Wyoming campus and the non-descript Fireside Bar and Lounge at 201 East Custer Street in Laramie, lies the Depression-era Albany County Courthouse.

A plain three-story structure built of light Wyoming sandstone, the courthouse was an unlikely candidate to become the center of worldwide attention for the issue of gay rights. But the deadly events of October 1998 meant the spotlight could not be avoided.

Inside the quiet courthouse, the case of two men accused of beating a young gay man to death would require massive preparations. President Bill Clinton and a variety of national figures had spoken out on the case—advocates for gay rights and those opposed to them quickly set up shop in Laramie. The Rev. Fred Phelps, pastor of the tiny Westboro Baptist "church" had made it his regular duty to vilify lesbians and gay men. He had made his presence known and told reporters his followers would be present for all proceedings in the case.

Outside the courthouse on Monday, April 5, 1999, a dozen gay rights advocates dressed "as angels with white sheets for wings" to block the view of anti-gay protestors from the Westboro Baptist Church. "The angels stood silently, but inside their human wall about a dozen anti-gay demonstrators shouted slogans and waved signs, including one that said, 'God hates fags.'"[366]

The AP reported, "The area outside the courthouse bustled with activity this morning and security was tight. . . . [and] about six [police] officers stood in a buffer zone between the two groups, and another officer videotaped the scene from atop the four-story courthouse. Temperatures hovered in the low twenties, but a wind made it feel colder as the two groups tried to outmaneuver each other. Shepard's supporters, under the name Angel Action, stood just in front of the protestors in an effort to block the view of people on Grand Avenue, the main street in front of the courthouse."[367]

The case to be heard was one intended to find justice for the brutal October 1998 beating and murder of Matthew Shepard, a twenty-two-year-old University of Wyoming student, whose homosexuality was a motivating factor in his attack. Shepard's body was discovered by a passing bicyclist on October 6, 1998 who at first "thought the crumpled form lashed to a ranch fence was a scarecrow. But when he stopped, he found the burned, battered and nearly lifeless body of Matthew Shepard."[368] Shepard died six days later from massive head wounds inflicted in the beating.

On October 16, 1998, funeral services were conducted for Shepard at St. Mark's Episcopal Church in Casper, Wyoming as a cold rain gave way to a wet, heavy snow and freezing temperatures. Regardless, the funeral quickly became a touchstone for both gay rights advocates and opponents. As *The Casper Star-Tribune* reported, "The much-anticipated clash between picketing anti-gay groups and 'anti-picketers' outside the memorial service for Matthew Shepard was peaceful, if sometimes loud and vulgar."[369]

Arrested and charged in the case were four other Laramie young adults, Russell Henderson, twenty-one years old, and Aaron McKinney, twenty-two, both charged with attempted murder and kidnapping. Two of their female friends, Kristen L. Price, eighteen, and Chastity V. Pasley, twenty, were charged as accessories after the fact for helping dump bloody clothing that would implicate Henderson and McKinney.

Charging information from Albany County Prosecutor Carlvin Rerucha indicated that Henderson and McKinney had "posed as homosexuals and lured Shepard out [of the Fireside Inn bar] to McKinney's pickup." Henderson reportedly told detectives about the ruse to lure Shepard from the bar, and that he had conceived of the idea, but that McKinney was the aggressor in the physical assault.

Police reported that before he was beaten, Henderson said he told Shepard, "Guess what, we're not gay. You're gonna get jacked."[370]

After luring Shepard from the bar, police said the two men beat Shepard inside the cab of the truck, and then tied him to a split-rail fence on Snowy Mountain View Road on the east edge of Laramie. He was also pistol whipped with the butt of a .357 magnum "while he begged for his life."[371]

Shepard's wallet and bank card were stolen—along with twenty dollars in cash he carried at the time of the attack.

The .357 was later recovered along with Shepard's wallet in McKinney's possession. Police disclosed the men took Shepard's shoes from him "so that he could not easily walk back into town" should he have freed himself from the fence. They needn't have worried, Shepard was near death from the moment they left him dangling from the fence.[372]

A bartender inside the Fireside Bar and Lounge, Jim Gregoire said he knew Shepard, Henderson and McKinney as regulars in the bar, but not young men who associated with one another.

"I knew Matthew, he was a real sweet, gentle person, he weighed all of 120 pounds," Gregoire said. "If I had seen him leave with those two guys [Henderson and McKinney], I would have stopped him. I wouldn't have let him go with them."[373]

From the start, media reports focused on Shepard's sexual orientation as a prime factor in his murder. *The Casper Star Tribune* reported the attack on Shepard as a hate crime.

The accused men were to be tried separately. Henderson's trial date was set for March 1999 as a tense set-up was unfolding at the stately Albany County Courthouse. Media reports indicated, "Unprecedented security" surrounded the case with "uniformed officers patrolling the four-story courthouse and grounds. Metal detectors screened visitors outside the building and again at the door of the third-floor courtroom of District Judge Jeffrey Donnell."[374]

Los Angeles Times writer Julie Cart noted, "Laramie is preparing as if for a siege. The stately stone courthouse has been belted by barricades and Judge Donnell has banned cameras from the courtroom."[375]

Cart correctly noted that Matthew Shepard "quickly became a national symbol of a hate crime victim. He was a bright, outgoing man who aspired to join the foreign service and work for human rights. But he was also troubled, according to friends. Shepard was hospitalized for depression [a year before his death] and took anti-anxiety medication. He eventually settled in Laramie, determined to attend his parent's alma mater and to flourish in the cocoon of a small town. Even with his mood swings, Shepard's most distinguishing trait appeared to be his likeability."[376]

As jury selection got underway, Henderson's attorney told prospective jurors the killing of Shepard "has literally injected into our community a feeling of guilt. The press wants us to think that we are somehow responsible for what went on October 6," said defense counsel Wyatt Skaggs. He asked jurors "Are any of you here going to judge this case because you feel guilty and want to make a statement to the nation?"—to which all replied "no."[377]

During his questioning of potential jurors, Skaggs declared, "This case is not about hate. All crimes aren't about hate. They all come down to some real simple motives."[378]

One prospective juror, a man in his forties, objected to Skaggs's characterization of the case. "No, I disagree," he said. "I think Matthew Shepard's lifestyle was part of this."[379]

Skaggs also said, "The defense will contend that Russell [Henderson] did not participate in the beating and did not share in the proceeds of the robbery."[380]

Skaggs could be outspoken in his approach—declaring before prospective jurors: "We've got to begin by disregarding the [personal] guilt thing, that we have to punish someone to show the nation we're not some dusty old cow town."[381]

Albany County Prosecutor Rerucha told jurors that while Shepard "was not the same as you and I" he still enjoyed equal protection under the Constitution.[382]

Unknown to protestors surrounding the courthouse and prospective jurors waiting inside the building, high-level negotiations had resulted in a deal that would stop the trial.

Attorneys for both sides announced Henderson would avoid trial and plead guilty to a charge of murder and kidnapping. In an afternoon hearing called for Henderson to enter his plea, he also apologized.

Looking at Matthew Shepard's parents in the courtroom, Henderson said, "Mr. and Mrs. Shepard, there is not a moment that goes by that I don't see what happened that night. I'm very sorry for what I did and I'm ready to pay my debt for what I did."[383]

He added, "You guys have my greatest sympathy for what happened."[384]

Judge Donnell declared Henderson's crime "vile and senseless" and that he deserved the most severe punishment possible. He was sentenced to two life terms without the possibility of appeal. Donnell told Henderson, "The court does not believe you feel any remorse. The pain you have caused here, Mr. Henderson, will never go away. Never."[385]

It was a sentiment later repeated by Judy Shepard who said she found Henderson's in-court statement inadequate. "At times, I don't know how you'd be worthy of any acknowledgement of your existence," Judy Shepard said in a shaking voice from a podium in the courtroom. "You murdered my son. None of us would be here today going through this agony if it wasn't for you."[386]

Turning to face Henderson, Mrs. Shepard said, "I hope you never experience a day or night without experiencing the terror, humiliation, hopelessness and helplessness my son felt that night."[387]

Dennis Shepard also spoke and addressed specifically Henderson's repeated claim that he was only a witness, and not a perpetrator. "It takes someone quite unique to sit and watch someone else be beaten to death and do nothing about it," Dennis Shepard said.[388]

Prosecutor Rerucha told reporters, "It is my hope that Mr. Henderson will die in the Wyoming state penitentiary and the only time he leaves the Wyoming state penitentiary is when they bury him."[389]

Henderson, now convicted, and his co-defendant McKinney (still awaiting trial) were everything Matthew Shepard was not. Both had come from broken homes and struggled in school. Both men scraped together a meagre living as roofers. Henderson's sad story grew even more so on January 3, 1999 as he awaited trial in the Shepard case when authorities announced his mother, forty-year-old Cindy Dixon, had "stumbled out of a Laramore bar and her frozen body was discovered the next day miles away along a country road."[390]

McKinney went to trial on his share of the charges in October 1999 as the one-year anniversary of the abduction and murder of Matthew Shepard approached. Prosecutors were seeking the death penalty against McKinney as attempts by his attorneys to get the death penalty off the table failed.

By now the Shepard case had become well-known national news, a Gannett News report carried nationwide reminding readers, "Bloody, unconscious and tied to a log fence of the edge of town, Shepard was found eighteen hours later by a jogger who thought he was a scarecrow. Five days later Shepard died in a hospital without regaining consciousness."[391]

Expected at the McKinney trial were gay rights advocates and those opposed to homosexuality, both of whom had become a regular feature as the case made its way through the criminal justice system. Also present were Shepard's parents, Dennis and Judy Shepard. News reports were now describing Judy Shepard as "a stay-at-home mother who became a vocal activist against hate crimes after her son's death. She now runs a foundation in his name and has appeared in a new documentary and a TV campaign against taunting of gays that is set to air on MTV."[392]

McKinney took the unusual step of talking via telephone to a reporter in June 1999, a potential violation of the judge's gag order in the case. From his jail cell he denied the motive for the crime had anything to do with Shepard's homosexuality and said, "I don't hate gay people."[393]

"The thing I don't like is people are saying it was a hate crime and I targeted him because he was gay," McKinney told a reporter from KGAB-TV via a telephone interview. McKinney expanded on his assertion: "I don't have anything against anybody. I don't hate gay people. I got a good friend that's gay. So I don't see where they're getting . . . just because he was gay they can go and say it was a hate crime and all this, when it wasn't. I think maybe people should have asked my side of the story before they went blowing it up, saying it was a hate crime and I targeted him because he was gay and all that nonsense. We didn't target anyone because they were gay. I had no idea Matthew Shepard was gay.[394]

While McKinney's interview was problematic, publicity around the case had been a problem during the earlier Henderson proceedings as well. One of his attorneys released a jailhouse letter written by someone named "A.M." to his wife in which he wrote, "Being a drunk homofobic [sic.] I flipped out and began to pistol whip the fag with my gun, ready at hand." Henderson may have hoped showing McKinney to be homophobic may have buttressed his argument that he was not an active participant in the murder.[395]

All McKinney would say to the KGAB reporter about his involvement in the case was, "Well, yeah, I had something to do with it."[396]

The evidence of his involvement was damaging to his defense—police recovered Shepard's wallet hidden in a baby's diaper inside an apartment McKinney shared with a girlfriend eight blocks away from the courthouse. The bloody gun used to beat Shepard was found in a pickup truck McKinney had borrowed from his father.

McKinney also told the TV reporter that beyond not holding hatred in his heart for anyone on the basis of "their race or sexual preference, or religion, or anything like that," he expressed "a little bit of fear" about facing the death penalty. "The death penalty would scare anybody, I would think," he said. "I think it is a little bit unfair."[397]

As the trial started, reporters focused on the transformation of the normally sleepy Laramie noting, "Surrounding the Albany County Courthouse, a three-story pile of sandstone block that sits between downtown Laramie and the University of Wyoming campus, is a chest-high, dark-green plastic fence containing rows of oblong holes. The fencing is the kind usually used to hold back the snow on ski slopes. But today, the beginning of the Aaron McKinney trial . . . the fence will be there to hold back the curious."[398]

While county officials prepared for large demonstrations, no one had yet applied for a permit to demonstrate. "People here hope to avoid scenes such as the one last year when antigay demonstrators descended on Shepard's funeral," *Philadelphia Inquirer* reporter Raad Cawthorn wrote.[399]

Cawthorn described Laramie as "pure west" in its look and feel, a city of 24,000 residents (about 10,000 of which are University of Wyoming students in town nine months of the year) unprepared for the role it was to play in the story of a gay young man martyred for his sexual orientation. He wrote, "Human rights activists quickly portrayed Shepard as a martyr and Laramie as a place where gay bashing was the inevitable byproduct of America's mythologizing of the cowboy."[400]

During opening statements, McKinney sat looking

downward as defense attorney Jason Tangeman told jurors that his client had been forced to perform oral sex on a neighborhood bully when he was just five-years-old. "Aaron will tell you this humiliated him horribly," Tangeman said, adding that he was again forced into homosexual acts by another man at age 15. Coupling McKinney's alleged history of sexual assault with his use of methamphetamine were factors to consider in his defense, Tangeman said.[401]

Considerable time was spent painting McKinney (and Henderson) as hard-luck high school dropouts who struggled for money, and sobriety with an aimless future ahead of them.

Tangeman infuriated Shepard's family and supporters when he mentioned that Matthew had asked McKinney for a ride home from the bar because he was too drunk to drive. He said McKinney believed Shepard was gay from the start.

"Why would Matthew Shepard ask for a ride home from strangers? We believe Matthew Shepard was looking for a sexual encounter" and alleged Shepard grabbed McKinney's genitals once he was on the front seat of the pick-up truck.[402]

In his open, prosecutor Cal Rerucha said the case before jurors "will simply be about the pain, suffering and death of [Matthew Shepard] at the hands of the defendant, Mr. McKinney."[403]

Prosecutors presented an emotional, but not particularly sympathetic case about Shepard. One state witness, Albany County Sheriff's Deputy Reggie Fluty testified about finding Shepard tied to the fence and near death. She told the barely breathing victim, "Baby, I'm so sorry this happened. . . . Hang in there son. Help is coming."[404]

Female jurors were witnessed weeping when shown graphic photos of the condition Shepard was found in by police, and his bloody clothes. Pathologists testified that his head wounds were sickeningly severe: Shepard had a broken nose, multiple skull fractures, and a damaged brain stem which led to unstoppable bleeding of the brain, causing death.

A bartender from the Fireside Lounge contradicted defense claims that Shepard was falling down drunk the night of the attack. Matt Galloway told jurors that Shepard appeared "at best, slightly buzzed," and that McKinney did not appear to be intoxicated at all.[405]

Trial proceedings ground to a halt on the third day of McKinney's trial when the judge, Barton Voigt, expressed (outside of the presence of the jury) concern about a proposed "gay panic" or "homosexual panic" defense McKinney's attorneys appeared to be approaching. "I don't know if I am going to allow such a defense," Voigt said, noting there was no provision for such an idea under Wyoming law.[406]

Despite having spent considerable time explaining how previous alleged homosexual assault incidents had rendered McKinney unable to control his emotions around gay men (and suggesting that Shepard had made a sexual pass to him), Dion Custis, one of McKinney's attorneys objected. "The only place [the gay panic defense idea] comes from is these people in the press," Curtis said, denying they were attempting such a move.[407] The judge eventually ruled defense attorneys could not use any so-called "gay panic" defense in the case—but could raise related issues in any subsequent sentencing phrase.[408]

When the trial resumed, the state called McKinney's girlfriend, Kristen Price, who was eight months pregnant with McKinney's son when the beating occurred. She testified that McKinney had told her, "A gay guy had been hitting on him in the bar. [McKinney and Henderson] decided in the bathroom to pretend they were gay, get him in the truck and rob him." A police detective confirmed that Henderson had told him upon his arrest that "some queer dude" had approached him and McKinney asking for a ride home.[409]

The state also played a videotaped statement McKinney gave police the morning he was arrested where he claimed Shepard "was grabbing my leg, grabbing my genitals, and I got pretty mad." He claimed he blacked out, but added, "It was like I could see what was going on, but somebody else was doing it."[410]

McKinney, although claiming that he blacked out, says he recalled Shepard begging for mercy and "he was all over me, trying to hug me" and "I was saying get away from me" as the brutal beating progressed.[411]

In his defense, McKinney's attorneys produced another man who was in the bar the night Shepard was beaten. He testified that Shepard came across as "blatantly gay" and had asked to join him at a table, uninvited.[412] Another witness was a former Cody, Wyoming bartender who admitted he knocked Shepard unconscious earlier in 1998 after he believed the young man made a homosexual pass at him.[413]

In closing arguments (despite denying he was using a "gay panic" defense argument), Custis persisted in efforts to say Shepard was attacked only because McKinney flew into an uncontrollable "gay rage." He said Shepard "was innocent, but he was also forward, and people reacted to that," Custis said. "We know you people may not like us trying to demean Matthew Shepard in any way, but don't hold that against Aaron McKinney."[414]

Albany County Prosecutor Cal Rerucha stuck to his main point, regardless of anyone's motivation, "Matthew Shepard was not an animal to be hung on a fence."[415]

Jurors returned guilty verdicts against McKinney, but before a sentencing hearing could go forward, Rerucha agreed to a requested meeting between McKinney and Shepard's parents. After that meeting, a deal was brokered whereby McKinney escaped the death penalty, but would remain imprisoned for life.

In court, Dennis Shepard spoke for his family and affirmed that his son's murder "was a hate crime, pure and simple. My son paid a terrible price to open the eyes of all of us who live in Wyoming, the United States and the world to the unjust and unnecessary fears, discrimination and intolerance that members of the gay community face every day."[416]

Dennis Shepard told the court, "Your honor, I would also like to thank you for the dignity and race with which this trial was conducted. Repeated attempts to distract the court from the true purpose of this trial failed because of your attentiveness, knowledge and willingness to take a stand and make new law in the area of sexual orientation and the 'gay panic' defense. By doing so, you have emphasized that Matthew was a human being with all the rights and responsibilities and protections of any citizen of Wyoming."[417]

"My son Matthew did not look like a winner," Dennis Shepard said. "After all, he was small for his age—weighing, at the most, 110 pounds, and standing only five feet two inches tall. He was rather uncoordinated and wore braces from the age of thirteen until the day he died. However, in his all too brief life, he proved that he was a winner. My son—a gentle, caring soul—proved that he was as tough as, if not tougher than anyone I have ever heard of or known."[418]

McKinney limited his remarks that he was "truly sorry" for his actions. "There won't be a day that goes by that I won't be ashamed for what I did, that's all."[419]

Laramie's Mayor Dave Williams said resolution of the cases provided "some relief" to the city. "We are not going to have reporters running 'round. We are not a community without problems, like any community. What [the case has done], more than anything else, is to have us take a look at ourselves. This crime is going to be etched in our minds for a long time."[420]

MOB VIOLENCE & JUSTICE

The South Faces a Troubled Reality

MADISON COUNTY COURTHOUSE

September 7, 1904—Huntsville, Alabama

Just four decades after the close of the Civil War, race relations remained quite strained across the South and anti-lynching advocates such as pioneering African-American journalist Ida B. Wells continued to gain support in many portions of the nation in response.

Five years before the National Association for the Advancement of Colored People (NAACP) was formed in 1909—and took the lead on calling the nation's attention to lynching in the South (and the North)—the leaders of Alabama attempted to hold lynchers accountable.

A 1904 lynching in Huntsville, Alabama offered a familiar story. A black man, Horace Maples, was arrested and charged with the murder of a popular local white citizen, John Waldrop. While he awaited trial at the Madison County Jail, a lynch mob was formed to subject Maples to vigilante justice.

"After setting fire to the jail and smoking out the prisoner while the fire department was held at bay with guns, and the sheriff and his deputies outwitted, a mob estimated at over 2,000 persons lynched Horace Maples . . . by stringing him to a tree on the courthouse lawn" on September 7, 1904, the Associated Press reported in a matter-of-fact manner.[421]

The action was taken despite speeches by community leaders asking local residents to remain calm. "The crowd began to gather Wednesday afternoon and night, as soon as the details of the crime spread throughout the country in which Waldrop [the murder victim] had a number of friends," an Associated Press report indicated.[422]

Acting Alabama Governor Russell McWhortor Cunningham ordered troops from Birmingham to Huntsville, 105 miles north. By the time the troops reached Huntsville, "the mob had swelled to enormous proportions."[423]

"While the sheriff and his deputies pluckily stood their guard, they were powerless before the mob and the fire," newspaper accounts indicated. "The local military company was called out, but they were outwitted by the men, who conceived of the idea of smoking out the prisoner."[424]

The arson fire, started at the back of the jail, burned quickly "with dense smoke spreading through the upper stories and cells of the building. The fire department was not allowed to approach within a block of the scene and was driven away with bullets."[425]

The sheriff and his deputies held out, refusing to release Maples, "but in some manner, the Negro got out [of the burning jail] through a window and jumped out of the building into a crowd. He was chased down and a rope thrown around his neck, and he was pulled up to the county courthouse. There was an immense crowd on the [courthouse] lawn."[426]

Eyewitness statements would later call into question whether Maples had jumped from the jail, or was, in fact, released by the sheriff in order to save the building from destruction by fire.

Witness reports said Maples "confessed" his crime and implicated two other black men. Madison County Solicitor Earl Pettus "delivered an impassioned address, trying to dissuade the mob. He was hooted down in turn."[427] US District Judge Shelby attempted to intervene as well by ordering the names of as many men as could be identified in the mob be written down.

Ignoring all of these entreaties, the angry men present grabbed Maples, threw a rope over a limb "and drew him up. The Negro was dead in a few minutes."[428]

Northern newspapers and African-American newspapers were highly critical of how the case had been handled. *The Rochester* (NY) *Democrat & Chronicle* noted, "The uselessness for practical purposes of the National Guard of southern states was again illustrated, this time at Huntsville, Alabama. . . . As it was taken for granted that the 'responsible citizens' of that section would not regret the opportunity to indulge in their favorite amusement, Negro lynching, which is to the South what bull fighting is to Spain. . . . The amusement seekers gathered in due course and after the usual period of preliminary howling went after the Negro who was to furnish the entertainment."[429]

The northern editorial writer noted, "What were the valuable soldiers of the state of Alabama doing all this time? Nothing whatsoever. . . . They made no attempt to do their duty. . . . They lived up to the worthless citizen soldiery of the South."[430]

Despite the doubts expressed up North about what might come of the lynching, the Associated Press reported a week after the lynching, indictments *were* announced against Huntsville Mayor Thomas W. Smith and Madison County Sheriff Augustus D. Rodgers for "dereliction of duty" as well as charges against twenty-six other men for lynching Maples. The AP dispatch offered ominously, "Further trouble is now feared" and members of the state militia were again ordered to Huntsville in response.[431]

Charles P. Lane, identified as the foreman of the grand jury, issued a statement amidst the growing tension that did little to calm feelings: "If the grand jury, in their wisdom and discretion, see fit to impeach the high sheriff of Madison County and his honor, the mayor of the city of Huntsville, for failure to discharge their duty in executing the law, we desire to do it legally."[432]

Lane's statement "created a sensation" and courthouse observers predicted more violence if the warrants for the sheriff and mayor were attempted to be served, and they were arrested. "In fact, open threats have been made that if certain persons are arrested, their friends will take them out of jail," the Associated Press relayed.[433]

Peace prevailed, however, as Alabama National Guard troops ordered to guard the jail prevented any new violence. News of the events in Huntsville continued to make headlines across the nation (especially since local officials were facing criminal charges in the matter).[434]

On September 21, 1904, prosecutors attempted to undertake a trial for the first man accused of participating in the lynching—Thomas R. Riggs—but were stymied by finding more than sixty potential jurors in the county who said they could not convict a man on a charge of murder for participating in a lynching. Riggs, one of twenty-six white men indicted in the case, was eventually acquitted as were three others where trials were held. The mayor and sheriff were also eventually cleared, with Smith elected to subsequent terms as mayor.[435]

Meanwhile, news also surfaced that the military planned to court martial certain members of the Huntsville militia for failing to act when the lynching occurred. Several officers were dismissed and the militia was ordered to be reassembled with new members.

A federal grand jury was assembled in late October 1904, and returned twelve separate federal indictments against local Huntsville citizens. The jurors wrote in their report that, "Something must be done to stop the frequent lynching's and outbreaks of anarchy in the South and that good citizens will welcome the punishment of mob leaders, whether by the federal court or the state court." Further, they encouraged more vigorous local law enforcement, "Otherwise there will be no protection for the life or property of citizens. The grand jury expresses the opinion that if Maples had been a white man accused of murdering a Negro would not have been lynched, therefore the lynchers showed conclusively to the grand jury that they were actuated by race prejudice."[436]

A Second Lynching After a Mistaken First

CHICKASAW COUNTY COURTHOUSE

February 8 and 9, 1913—Houston, Mississippi

One of the least examined, but most disturbing lynchings to ever occur was actually two lynchings in two days, with two black men taken to their death by vigilante mobs determined to do their will.

The setting is a familiar one, the courthouse square at the center of a small town, this one carrying a big-city name: Houston, Mississippi. Bounded by Jefferson, Jackson, Madison and Washington streets, the new courthouse, first opened in 1909 was small but radiated the type of dignity the architects, builders and county fathers likely sought. The small community of Houston, situated about forty miles southeast of Tupelo, was home to barely 1,000 people:

> None of the town's pride was present, it seems, however, on a violent, bloody weekend in early February 1913—two separate lynchings overtaking any criminal justice processes the courthouse could contain.

The trouble started when the body of the young wife of a county official, Mrs. Bessie (Farr) Williams, was found in "an abandoned pit at her home. Robbery is believed to have been the motive for the crime, as a diamond ring which Mrs. Williams wore was missing." Bessie was the wife of the deputy county clerk John Clifton Williams whom she had married just over two months earlier.

The New Orleans Times-Democrat and many other southern newspapers ran a detailed account of the alarming story, "Bride Found Murdered." Declaring Mrs. Williams' murder "The most brutal crime ever committed in Chickasaw County. . . . [Mrs. Williams was killed] as she was at home preparing dinner 10:30 or 11 o'clock this morning when the circumstances show the murderer attacked her in the living room of the house, choked her and beat her with some blunt instrument, supposed to be a fire poker, as this was broken when found," the AP reported.[437]

"Mrs. Williams fell near the fire and her left hand was burned severely," the dramatic account continued. "The murderer took a diamond solitaire ring and the diamonds from a brooch. He carried the body through the house and out the kitchen door and threw it in an old pit under the kitchen and closed the door to the pit. He then pulled down all the shades in the house and closed all the doors."[438]

John Williams came home from the courthouse for lunch, could not find his wife, but did find evidence of blood in the living room and a trail of blood in the kitchen which he said he followed to the pit.

Two witnesses, described in newspaper accounts as either "two Negro women" or "Negresses," said they saw a black man near the home of the victim the day she was slain.[439] Police quickly focused on one suspect, "A certain Negro who lives about 30 yards from the kitchen door of the Williams' home" immediately after the body was found.[440]

While the sheriff attempted to undertake his investigation, it was clear some local residents weren't willing to wait for the official process to take its course. "Tonight, at a mass meeting of almost the entire population of the town and adjoining county, ten Negroes and two white men were put through vigorous 'sweating' without blame for the murder being fixed," a reporter from Houston, Mississippi noted.[441]

"Other Negroes under arrest have been threatened," an Associated Press report indicated suggesting a "race war" was at hand. "There is grave danger of a pitched battle and blacks armed with repeating rifles and shotguns are pouring into Houston. The Negro quarter is an armed camp."[442]

Less than twenty-four hours after the murder, the sheriff had arrested two black men, Andrew Williams and David Rucker, although it was not clear if both were implicated in the murder and robbery. Local vigilantes were not waiting to sort it out—they set upon Williams at the Chickasaw County Jail.

"When the mob attempted to take Williams from the jail where he was confined [just after five p.m. on Saturday, February 8], he offered desperate resistance but was finally dragged from the building and lynched to a tree near the courthouse. The Negro refused to make a confession and declined to make any other statement other than, 'You will do the same to me if I tell you the truth that you will do if I don't.'"[443]

Newspaper accounts indicated that Andrew Williams was

first hung from a telephone pole near the jail, rather than at the courthouse. From the start, however, many believed the mob had grabbed the "wrong" man—leaving thirty-year-old David Rucker in the jail. Rucker's safety would soon be in danger, however.

As *The Atlanta Constitution* reported, as Sunday, February 9 rose on Houston, "A mob of one thousand persons conducted a mock trial in the courthouse yard here today [for Rucker] . . . in the presence of a sheriff and two deputies who were powerless to act."[444]

As ugly as the lynching of Williams had been a day earlier, a terribly troubling description of the second event indicated that the mob chained Rucker to a "still pump in the middle of the [courthouse] yard, soaked his clothes with oil, piled wood about him and burned him alive."[445] Rucker was the second black man to die for the murder of Mrs. Williams. "A mob hanged a Negro named Andrew Williams the day before for the same crime, but his innocence has been established." Early news reports misidentified Andrew Williams as "Jim Jones"—but the result was the same.[446]

Subsequent accounts of Rucker's lynching indicated a profoundly disturbing scene playing out on the courthouse lawn. "[Rucker] was taken to the [courthouse] square and chained to an iron post," a later Associated Press report said. "A kettle of tar was poured over him and faggots [lit torches] were piled about him. He was allowed to talk for a short time [and then] a brother of Mrs. Williams touched a match to the dry wood. Rucker had scarcely begun to feel the effects of the heat when the father of Mrs. Williams [the murder victim] elbowed his way through the throng and shot him four times."[447]

As would often be the case, the story emanating from tiny Houston seemed to evolve. An AP wire story moved the day after the lynching indicated that a court stenographer was summoned from the courthouse to take town Rucker's "confession" prior to his hanging.

Observers noted the mob was "determined to give Rucker a public trial" after taking him from the jail by force "without official interference. He was led down the street to a convenient open spot, the court stenographer summoned, and an opportunity given the Negro to tell his story. He was quizzed for two hours."[448]

Those present said Rucker blamed Andrew Williams, the man lynched the day before, for the killing, but under continual questioning began to implicate himself. "At the conclusion [of Rucker's 'testimony'], the question of punishment was debated. 'Burn him!' someone laconically said, and Rucker was marched to the courthouse yard where he was bound to the pump," *The Jackson Daily News* reported.[449]

The Chickasaw County district attorney attempted, in vain, to cause the mob to stand down and assured them he had spoken to Mississippi Governor Earl L. Brewer by telephone and that a special court session would be ordered immediately to properly try Rucker. "The crowd listened respectfully, but proceeded with its preparation to execute the prisoner," witnesses reported.[450] The sheriff and his deputies apparently were unwilling to take any action, a reporter noting that they were "under guard inside the courthouse [and] witnessed the scene through a window."[451]

In Jackson, the governor told reporters he had received a request for troops but it was received too late to intercede in the lynching of Rucker.[452] "Governor Brewer was loath to believe that there would be further mob action, and was in hopes that the temper of the outraged citizens would cool down with the passing of another day," *The Vicksburg Evening Post* told its readers.[453]

The final reports on the ugly matters in Houston noted that after Rucker was lynched, "The ashes were gathered up and carried away, and the crowd dispersed."[454]

"The Center Hanging Tree"

SHELBY COUNTY COURTHOUSE

August 2, 1920 and May 21, 1928—Center, Texas

Photo courtesy of L. A. Turner

A southern red oak tree on the south lawn of the Shelby County Courthouse in tiny Center, Texas became so famous, it was known for generations as "the Center Lynching Tree."

On that site, on two separate occasions separated by eight years in the 1920s, two black men met their death at the hands of mob justice that was unwilling to wait for the regular wheels of justice to turn. The town of Center, just seventeen miles southwest of the Texas-Louisiana border created by the Sabine River, would produce two troubling stories that many locals would rather forget.

On the hot, sunbaked day of August 2, 1920, mob justice reared its head for the first time as more than 1,000 men stormed the Shelby County Jail, broke through a steel door and dragged seventeen-year-old Lige Daniels from his cell. Daniels, described in newspaper reports as "a Negro prisoner," was being held on a charge of murder in the death of Maggie Hall, the forty-two-year-old widow of a local farmer.

Mrs. Hall's death had been a violent one, and when news emerged that Daniels had allegedly confessed to the killing before both the District Attorney and members of the county's sitting grand jury, it appeared violence was at hand.

"The wife of the farmer was brutally attacked and later found unconscious near her home," the AP reported. "Her skull was crushed and her body bruised. She was brought to a local sanitarium, dying. The Negro confessed to the [grand] jurors that he had brutally attacked the woman, he had hacked her head with a hoe."[455]

Within an hour of his confession, Daniels was hanging dead from a courthouse tree.

The Texas Calvary was called to help protect Daniels "but was unable to find any members of the company in time for mobilization."[456]

The crowd responsible for the violence quickly dispersed after the lynching. It was the second attempt to lynch Daniels, the previous mob being talked down by District Attorney J. P. Anderson and Judge Spottswood Sanders who assured them a speedy trial would occur. Locals were concerned, however, since at age seventeen, Daniels was not eligible for the state's death penalty and faced a lighter sentence because he was officially still a juvenile.

One of the initial newspaper dispatches from Center reported in Shreveport, Louisiana, about 65 miles away, expressed optimism that a lynching could be prevented. "As the jail is strongly built, it is expected to take the mob an hour or longer to accomplish its task unless the authorities as indicated are able to prevent it."[457]

The optimism was poorly placed as Daniels was quickly seized and killed.

Following the ugly scene, Judge Sanders urged that indictments be brought against all those responsible for killing Daniels. No indictments or convictions were ever secured, however.

Before his arrest for the murder of Mrs. Hall, Daniels was known to local authorities. "The Negro has figured before the court for the last several years," *The Marshall News Messenger* reported. "Last spring he was charged with the burning of the Lawrence Scruggs residence near Center, and in a statement just before he was hung he is alleged to have said that his only regret was that he could not get several others."[458]

The tree on which Daniels died, which quickly became known as "the Center Hanging Oak," stood on the south lawn of the courthouse, facing Austin Street.

"While a young boy climbed the tree to assist in placing a rope over a stout limb, the men stood with their noosed captive on a set of wooden steps," according to a website for famous trees researched by the Texas A&M University Forest Service. "After the rope was tied off and before the steps were removed, a court official mounted the scaffold to plead with the mob to stop. His plea was cut short when the makeshift scaffold collapsed and all on it but [Daniels] landed on the ground."[459]

Texas historian Dilip D'Souza described the lynching scene based on a widely distributed photograph of the event: Daniels was "wearing a white shirt, torn pants and no shoes, his head tilted back sightlessly, this black teenager hung that day from the limb of a tree." A photograph of the incident was offered as a postcard, which D'Souza said showed "a mass of white men, many looking at the camera and milling about. The camera catches one boy, possibly twelve or thirteen years old, looking up at the lynched seventeen-year-old. His smile and glee at the scene are clear. It's probably the best fun he has had all that long, hot summer vacation from school."[460]

A second hanging occurred at Center on May 21, 1928—bringing the death of Eolis "Buddy" Evans who was accused of a May 12, 1928 assault on a local man, John T. Wheeler. Wheeler was allegedly struck on the head with a piece of lumber, and died later. Evans, who had escaped twice from local jails, was taken from deputies as they attempted to return him to the Shelby County Jail.

"He was hanged from the same oak tree in the courthouse yard where another Negro was lynched about five years ago," the Associated Press reported.[461]

Evans was removed at gunpoint from deputies at about 5:30 p.m. on Saturday evening after he had been recaptured hours earlier from his second jail escape. As they returned him to Center, deputies "were overpowered by a mob of between 200 or 300 white men who took the Negro and with little ceremony hanged him from the limb of a courthouse tree."[462]

Texas Governor Dan Moody said Texas State Rangers were available to assist in Center, if needed, although no request for their help had been made. "Whether any official action would be taken against any members of the mob was not known," *The Waco News-Tribune* reported. "The matter had not been brought before Governor Moody, who was attending the State Democratic Convention at Beaumont. Center officers said they could take no action, as no complaints had been filed with them."[463]

After the Daniels lynching, one local man saved the rope used to hang the man and displayed it as a prominent "decoration" for his front porch. Another collected the limb from the tree and made gavels of the wood. The tree later died and was eventually removed in 1990.

In 2015, Allan Turner, an Associated Press writer, revisited the history of Center's two horrible lynching incidents. "They've cut down the lynching tree on town square," Turner wrote. "It has no place in modern, progressive Center, a Shelby County hamlet just seventeen miles from the Louisiana line. . . . Today, Center residents, white and black, like to describe their town, population 5,100, as a sylvan paradise where 'big city blues melt away.'"[464]

A Deadly Defense of the Courthouse

FAYETTE COUNTY COURTHOUSE

February 9, 1920—Lexington, Kentucky

The random murder of a ten-year-old Kentucky girl would always incite the interest and consternation of the community, but it was especially so in February 1920 when police arrested a black man and charged him with the senseless crime.

Geneva Hardeman was supposed to be on her way to school on the morning of February 4, 1920 but never made it there. A local citizen picked up her book satchel along the road, and carried it to the local schoolhouse, thinking a child had dropped it en route to school. Geneva was absent from school, and a quick check with her mother found she was not there either. An immediate search was started.

Before long Geneva's battered and muddied body was found in a nearby cornfield beneath corn stalks piled loosely over her body in the South Elkhorn area of Fayette County. Police reported, "The physical evidence at the scene indicated 'a sharp struggle in the tramped mud,' a large rock covered in blood, and the young girl was covered in blood [as were the stalks about her] and a child's umbrella [bent in half at the handle]. One of her hair ribbons were tramped into the mud next to her body."[465]

Newspaper accounts told the story this way: "The little Hardeman girl was found murdered by schoolmates a short distance from her home last Tuesday morning, just a few minutes after she had left home for a nearby schoolhouse. She had been dragged into a cornfield and her head had been crushed with a shovel. The body had been partly covered up with corn stalks."[466]

Sheriff's deputies employed bloodhounds and via a circuitous route eventually settled upon William Lockett, a thirty-two-year-old black man, as their suspect. Witnesses placed Lockett in the area before and after the girl disappeared, but details of why Lockett was the suspect were scant. Reports surfaced that Lockett had confessed to the crime, but were contradicted later by other reports that he had not confessed.

Community outrage grew quickly as details of the case spread, and before nightfall, some citizens were demanding a form of "vigilante justice" be taken against Lockett. "A mob formed at the Fayette County Jail at Lexington last night, and a committee was permitted to inspect the prison to convince themselves that Lockett was not there," United Press International reported. "The rioters than commandeered automobiles and followed Sheriff Moore and his prisoner to Frankfort. On the hill overlooking the prison, the sheriff blocked the road with automobiles, stopping the pursuit. After an hour's argument, he persuaded the mob to return to Lexington."[467]

Once Lockett was held at the state prison at Frankfort (about twenty-five miles from Lexington), the UPI reported that 100 riot guards were stationed there to prevent any attempt to lynch Lockett. Lockett would remain jailed at Frankfort as tensions continued to run high back in Lexington.

On the following Monday, February 9, 1920, Lockett was returned under heavy guard to the Fayette County Courthouse in Lexington for trial. Kentucky Governor Edward P. Morrow authorized Kentucky National Guard troops for the transport and protection of Lockett to prevent any attempts at "lynch justice." In Downtown Lexington, the troops lined the streets from the jail to the courthouse in order to safely transport Lockett to trial, and citizens were warned that troops would "shoot to kill" anyone who attempted to break their lines. Despite the warning, some "hand-to-hand combat" was reported between citizens and troops.

At the Fayette County Courthouse, Judge Charles Kerr was determined to go forward with the trial, but to do so quickly. Outside the courthouse, however, tensions continued to mount.

"While the brief trial was in progress, a mob of 4,000 persons gathered," the Associated Press reported. "Surrender of the Negro was demanded, and the mob began advancing toward the courthouse. A company of state militia, reinforced by overseas soldiers in iron helmets, ordered the crowd back. Suddenly, a voice in the middle of the mob yelled, 'Let's go now!' The crowd surged up the steps of the courthouse. A deputy sheriff arrested one of the leaders and led him away. Officers with pistols threatened to shoot if necessary."[468]

Rioters continued and tried to take guns from the militia members. Finally, an order to fire was given and when the shooting stopped, "three men fell dead on the courthouse steps. Others carried them to the rear. Another fell as the struggle continued. Machine guns crackled and the crowd broke for cover."[469]

National Guard troops were under the command of Adjutant General James M. Deweese who explained, "No shots were fired until the crowd had reached the machine guns. I backed up twenty steps, grappled with two of the leaders, striking one over the head with my pistol. The volley which stopped the rush was not fired a second too soon."[470]

A bizarre scene played out that day in Lexington. As machine gun fire was opened up on mobbing citizens at the courthouse door, "the trial of Lockett was proceeding in the courthouse. In fifteen minutes he was sentenced to death."[471] The jury deliberated in the courtroom and did so with little discussion.

"Inside the courtroom, the trial was interrupted by the shots [outside the courthouse], but the deputies maintained order. One man entered the courtroom shouting, 'Judge, you'd better let them have this man. They coming up here and they'll kill a lot of men.' He was ejected. The trial took only thirty-five minutes, including the interruption by gun fire."[472]

Although the courtroom was packed for Lockett's trial—and everyone attending was searched for weapons before being allowed to be seated—accounts of the trial were as brief as the trial itself. After the state made its case, the defense consisted almost entirely of reminding jurors that Lockett was a veteran of World War I and had been stationed at Camp Taylor in Louisville.

"I don't know why I did it," Lockett was quoted to the jury.[473] Lockett was a resident of Henderson, Kentucky. Although an Army veteran, prosecutors said he was also well known to local police as an alleged bootlegger and burglar.

Some described Lockett as almost incoherent in his spoken communication; however, his defense attorney released a cogent statement from his client at the time of trial. "I know I do not deserve mercy, but I am sorry I committed the crime and I would give anything if the little girl could be brought back to life."[474]

Outside the courthouse, while three men were reported dead at the scene, two others died later and were among about fifteen wounded persons carried from the scene by members of the mob. Two women were reported to be among those injured. News stories identified the dead men (all white) as J. M. Rogers, John Thomas and William Ethrington, all of Versailles (a rural Woodford County community about fifteen miles west of Lexington); along with B. F. Carrier and L. M. King of Lexington. A sixth victim was identified as "an unidentified Negro girl."[475]

Following the fracas, 400 additional troops from Camp Taylor, Kentucky were ordered to Lexington. "Soldiers and policemen continued on guard near the courthouse following the shooting," the AP reported. "Officials feared another attempt might be made to lynch Lockett."[476] Amazingly, during the riot, police were able to slip Lockett from the courthouse and return him to a prison cell in Frankfort.

The day after the riot, the Associated Press reported, "Dawn today found Lexington an armed camp. Squads of armed soldiers who saw service [in World War I] were patrolling the streets or guarding all the approaches to the city to prevent a recurrence of yesterday's mob violence that cost the lives of five persons and caused injury to a score of others."[477]

Lexington was under martial law during these days and "Soldiers were posted about the courthouse. . . . Soldiers search every person in the streets after dark. The veterans were posted on each road leading to Lexington, and entrance to the city was refused."[478]

The Commonwealth of Kentucky waited the minimum of thirty days before scheduling Lockett for execution, the fastest they were allowed to do so under existing law. Just before he was executed, however, Lockett made startling disclosures not only about the murder of the Hardeman girl, but also about the murder of four other women in three states since 1905. Lockett, who said his birth name was Petrio Kimbrough, reportedly told Prison Warden John B. Chilton that "when he steps into the electric chair March 11, he wants to feel he is paying the penalty for all and not just one of his crimes."[479]

Lockett said he killed his first victim, a white woman in Todd County, Kentucky in December 1905; killed another woman near Carmi, Illinois in 1912; killed a black woman in Evansville, Indiana in 1917; and in February 1919 (while still in the Army) implicated himself in the murder of a woman near Camp Taylor, Kentucky.

"He says he does not know whether [his last victim] was white or black," the Associated Press reported. "He later says a skeleton was found near the spot where he hid the body, and authorities said it was that of a Negro woman."[480]

All of his victims were strangled.

Lockett was put to death in the commonwealth's electric chair on March 11, 1920 at the state penitentiary at Eddyville, Kentucky, a reporter noting, "The electric chair at the state penitentiary here exacted the vengeance denied a mob which sacrificed six lives at Lexington in February."[481] Among those who witnessed the execution were two brothers and two uncles of the Hardeman girl—four of twenty men from Fayette County allowed to witness the execution.

"Lockett walked to the death chamber with steady step at 4:10 a.m. He said nothing as he entered the chamber, but watched the guards intently. The first shock was given at 4:14, followed by a second of 21,000 volts at 4:20."[482] Lockett was pronounced dead at 4:32 a.m.

Lockett reportedly did make a plea for clemency for two other men awaiting execution, Charles Douthitt and Hoe Hughes. Warden Chilton released a statement some doubted actually came from Lockett, but offered, "I am ready to die now anytime the court wants me to whether it be in a week or thirty days . . . I am sorry I did it. I'm spending all my time praying and reading the Bible and I know I will be prepared to go when the time comes for me to die. I hope I will be forgiven."[483]

The "Last Northern" Lynching in America

GRANT COUNTY COURTHOUSE
August 7, 1930—Marion, Indiana

In the summer of 1930, the Grant County Courthouse square in Marion, Indiana looked like the ninety-one other county seats across the state—large shade trees framing the proud courthouse and providing a park-like atmosphere around the seat of government. Today, only two trees remain on the lawn of the courthouse—neither of them old enough to hold the history of the one that brought a generation of shame upon this northern community.

On a hot and humid summer night, August 7, 1930, two black men accused in the killing of a local man and the molest of his girlfriend, were pulled from the jail and hung from trees on the northeast corner of the courthouse square—near Third and Adams streets.

The two men, J. Thomas Shipp, eighteen years old, and Abraham S. Smith, ninteen—described in media reports as "two youthful Negroes"—were held on a charge of murder in the death of Claude Deeter, twenty-three, of Fairmount and the alleged rape of his eighteen-year-old girlfriend, Mary Ball. Deeter and Ball were reported accosted as they sat in a car on a well-known "lover's lane" on the east side of Marion.

An Associated Press dispatch from Marion reported, "Mob violence apparently had cooled today after a frenzied demonstration last night in which two ninteen-year-old Negroes were taken from the Grant County Jail by a mob and lynched on the lawn of the county courthouse."[484]

Further details indicated, "Although crowds of several hundred persons milled about the bodies throughout the night preventing officials from removing them, the heat of the angry mob seemed to cool past Midnight and police and county authorities expressed no fear of further outbreaks."[485]

After the ugly deed was completed, Grant County Coroner O. L. Stout and Sheriff James C. Campbell attempted to remove the bodies at Midnight, "but the crowd resented this, demanding that they remain aloft. The authorities were content with this lest further outbreaks occur. The bodies were not removed until 6 o'clock [the following morning]."[486] The county coroner later determined the men died of strangulation, but also had been severely beaten.[487]

Estimates of the crowd size varied widely—from 5,000 to 20,000 people—although most were simply curious onlookers. Sirens from the fire trucks—called out to try to use fire hoses to disperse the crowd (when tear gas failed)—brought out even more inquisitive residents.

The original mob of several hundred men reportedly formed about nine p.m. eleven miles away from the courthouse in Fairmount, a small community in the southern part of the county (a town eventually made famous by a young man named James Dean born there in February 1931). Rumors throughout the day indicated mob violence was possible, but Sheriff Campbell said he was confident no such outbreak would occur—nothing like that had ever happened in Marion before.

Regardless, once in Marion, the Fairmount men were joined by morc locals who were determined to take matters into their own hands. "Forty or fifty of the leaders, chiefly younger men, pried away the giant lock of the outer jail door and made their way to the Sheriff's door and made their way to [Thomas] Shipp's cell on the first floor," the AP reported. "Cellmates attempted to shield him by boosting him into a chute, but failed."[488]

"Shipp at first begged for mercy, but then fought fiercely when the mob would not listen," the AP report said. Smith, housed on the third floor of the jail, was pulled from his cell next. Originally, the mob planned to hang the men from a tree at the jail, but changed their mind and dragged them the short distance to the courthouse.[489]

"One of the colored men . . . was still alive when his body was swung into the air and he is said to have clutched at the rope with his hands," media reports indicated. After this, members of the mob took a large board and broke both of his arms to prevent any further resisting.[490]

A third young black man pulled from the jail, sixteen-year-old James Cameron was saved only when someone in the mob declared he was not involved with the other two men's crimes. Sheriff Campbell appealed to the angry group to leave Cameron, and was quoted as saying, "You have your two men now, that should satisfy you."[491]

Campbell's jail guards were no match for the crowd—even with the help of all twenty-eight officers of the Marion City Police Department. Tear gas canisters fired to disperse the crowd were thrown back at the officers, and even firefighters were threatened if they attempted to hook up fire hoses.

Campbell worked the phones (in the years before station-to-station police radios were in place) and put out a call for help. Responding officers came from the Indiana State Police, as well as city and county officers from nearby Muncie, Kokomo, Anderson, Wabash, Huntington, Alexandria, and Hartford City. Regardless, "they were able to do little to suppress the crowd. No shots were fired during the entire proceeding."[492]

The grizzly details of the events were hard to take: "The bodies were stripped of nearly all their clothing before they were hung. . . . Although presenting a ghastly sight, large crowds including many women and children milled about the bodies, some of them taking souvenirs."[493] Witnesses said citizens had slit the legs of the trousers of one of the victims and tore away bits of the cloth, as much as could be reached from the ground. Others broke off twigs and limbs from the tree.[494]

Sheriff Campbell told reporters that when it appeared the lynching rumors were true, and a mob was approaching the jail, he attempted to remove all of the black prisoners from the jail to move to another city but found "the tires on his car were flat, and the gasoline had been drained from the tank."[495]

Campbell claimed his only victory was helping to prevent the mob from moving to the "Negro section of city"—known as the Johnston neighborhood. The sheriff addressed a frightened and angry crowd of about 500 black citizens there, and with the help of outside police agencies, kept peace and order in that area.

The Kokomo Tribune reported, "Havoc and tragedy, charged to an infuriated mob, greeted the eyes of those who paid early morning visits to the city of Marion Friday. Grim evidence of the struggles of the night, in which two colored men were hanged in the courthouse yard, were still plainly visible."[496]

Kokomo Police Chief Clinton Jackson said, "I doubt if we could have done much if all of us had been there all the time. When we arrived, we found the streets alive with people. Traffic was so heavy in the business district to make the streets impassable. Crowds milled about the jail and the courthouse. We had expected to find a sullen, dangerous mob. Instead, we were surprised to find everyone apparently in good humor. Everybody we met seemed good natured and greeted us with shouts of, 'Well, you got here too late!'"

In the aftermath of the shameful events, Grant County Prosecutor Harley Hardin said he was inclined to take no immediate action. "The Grant County grand jury will be called to convene when the fall term of the court opens on September one, and its duty will be to inquire into the events of the last few days. Grant County officials are law-abiding and perform their duty regardless of any temporary influences," he said.

Hardin, understanding that the event was making the community look awful not only across Indiana, but the nation, quickly added, "As a whole, Grant County citizens respect law and order and they may have confidence that justice will be done to the fullest extent."[497]

Hardin said as many as twenty names had been forwarded to him as being chiefly responsible for the violence. He cautioned, however, "I feel sure that indictments may be obtained, but convictions look doubtful to me."[498]

Hardin said his office had also officially requested that local portrait photographer Lawrence Beitler cease from selling any more copies of the "flashlight photograph" he took of the dead men hanging from the courthouse tree. "The police said that the gruesome pictures, which were being sold by the hundreds, were stirring up an intense feeling which might develop into a dangerous situation," the Associated Press reported.[499]

The photograph by Beitler was widely distributed across the nation, including on post cards and newspaper wires. The moment captured by Beitler, with white residents casually milling about the two dead men's bodies hanging from trees, was a quintessential image of lynching in America. Eventually, the image was even included in a French book discussing American history.

Indiana Attorney General James M. Ogden said, "There is no doubt that such an affair gives the state a black eye and generally should be deplored. You know they who 'sow the whirlwind reap the storm.'"[500]

The state's governor, Harry G. Leslie, was out of the state on a fishing trip to Canada at the time of the attack and could not immediately be notified of the events, his aides said. They estimated he was in such a remote area of Canada that it would take at least one day for the governor to reach a telephone to receive the news.

The night after the lynching, "The city was quiet, but it was well guarded against possible recurrence of trouble with patrols of 130 state militia soldiers and twenty-five state policemen. Officials believed that the crisis in the tenseness would pass tonight and but little fear was expressed of any further uprising."[501]

Despite the peacefulness, the downtown streets of Marion remained busy with automobile and foot traffic. "Lured by curiosity, large crowds were on the streets [of Marion] tonight to view the large elm tree where the mob hanged its victims and the county jail, which was undergoing repairs to its locks and doors which were broken down by the frenzied mob,"[502] the Associated Press reported.

The Marion Chronicle declared in an editorial the day after the lynching that the mob was "spurred on to its violent act by a want of confidence in the processes of the courts. . . . The men who last night broke into the jail and took two self-confessed criminals out and hanged them would not have been prompted to act had it not been that there was no assurance that the two youths, guilty of an atrocious act and the murder of one of their fellow citizens, would have paid the penalty for their crime."[503]

The National Association for the Advancement of Colored People (NAACP) issued a statement on the events at Marion: "We profoundly regret the unfortunate event of the past few days, deploring deeply that in the fair state of Indiana people could so far forget the honor due to law and order. The crime committed was deplorable and since the NAACP stands always for the enforcement of law and justice for all, it was our hope that justice through the courts might be meted out. The crime is without color or race, being an evil in all races."[504]

Months later, reporters at *The Indianapolis Star* took up the question of why the lynching had occurred, the last in the state's history, and at a time when most citizens thought the risk of such mob violence was over. Rather than focusing on the racial aspects of the trial—the suspects were black and the angry mob was white—*The Star* analysis indicated the lynching grew out of a perceived leniency in the Grant County courts in the preceding years.

The Star reported that court records in Grant County showed "excessive suspensions of sentences, unusually heavy dismissals of cases, and comparatively few prison commitments." Statistically, Grant County judges dismissed almost twice as many cases as any other county in the state for 1929, the newspaper reported. In addition, twenty-five percent of all penalties were suspended in Grant County in

1928—dramatically higher than a suspension rate of one-tenth of cases statewide.

Further analysis posited, "Adding fuel to the flames of discontent were long delays on appeals, rapid upshot in recent years in the number of murders in the county, and as Hardin opined, failure by Grant County juries to convict and their tendency to fix lenient sentences. Hardin added that a death penalty has never been fixed by a Grant County jury."[505]

At the end of December 1930, a trial began for seven men accused of participating in the lynching—but not via a local indictment, but instead from charges brought by Attorney General Ogden. Members of the Grant County grand jury called by Hardin declined to return any indictments.

The men accused in the case brought by Ogden were Robert Bershire, forty-five years old; Chester Pease, thirty-two; Philip Boyd, seventeen; Everett Clark, twenty-two; Asa Davis, twenty-two; Charles Lennon, thirty; and Arnold Waller, twenty-two. Under Indiana law in 1930, conviction for participation in a lynching could result in the death penalty, while being convicted of being present or abetting the action could result in a prison term.

In addition to the seven men accused, Grant County Sheriff Jacob C. Campbell was charged by Ogden with "neglect of duty" following the violence, but was still called as a witness against the accused men. He left office at the end of 1930.

Berkshire's trial was taken up first, and he was found not guilty by a Grant County jury after forty-five minutes of deliberation on January 2, 1931. Ogden would quickly grow frustrated with his inability to mete out any justice in Grant County for the lynching. Not only were none of the seven men indicted ever convicted, Sheriff Campbell was also acquitted of any negligence of duty.

Ogden, a graduate of Harvard University, had gained national attention and respect being elected president of the National Association of Attorneys General. A reported gubernatorial hopeful, he served as Attorney General from 1924 to 1931, a key period in Indiana history when the state had to face its racist and corrupt local government infrastructure. Just over a year after the Marion lynching, Ogden spoke before a statewide meeting of the NAACP in South Bend in October 1931 declaring, "Today, Marion is seething in corruption. Local authorities have failed completely in the prevention of bombings and lynchings, and the city presents a sorry tale of defeated justice. Mob rule has been allowed to supersede law, and its courts have fallen down."[506]

Historian James H. Madison wrote an extensive review of the case, *A Lynching in the Heartland: Race and Memory in America*, in which he attempted to keep focused on "the courthouse square of Grant County, Indiana, the community's geographic and symbolic center." He said the events in Marion were a "typical Midwestern courthouse [where] the reader can see the central themes of twentieth-century America played out in terms of ordinary people's lives." For the people of Grant County, "The lynching did not go away. Indeed, the stories, the memories, even some said, the collective guilt, increased as the community slouched toward the end of the twentieth century."[507]

Madison told a reporter at the time his book was released that "There is nothing insidious or malignant about Grant County that would explain such an unbelievable, unimaginable event, except to say there's a darkness in the human soul that came forth that night in Marion."[508]

The surviving young man in the case, James Cameron, eventually dedicated the rest of his life as a civil rights activist, helping start three chapters of the NAACP, and from 1942–50 serving as the director of the State of Indiana's Office of Civil Liberties. In 1988, he founded America's Black Holocaust Museum in Milwaukee, Wisconsin. In 1991, Indiana Governor Evan Bayh pardoned Cameron for his original charges. Cameron died in 2006 at the age of ninety-two.[509]

A Case of Burning Justice

GRAYSON COUNTY COURTHOUSE

May 9, 1930—Sherman, Texas

Photo courtesy of S. Hawkins

The alleged rape case brought to the district court at the Grayson County Courthouse in tiny Sherman, Texas in the spring of 1930 had all of the elements of a powder keg.

Sherman, Texas was a typical county seat town with a population in 1930 of about 15,000 inhabitants. Mostly an agricultural community, white tenant farmers were struggling to make a living in the county, a fact confirmed by the Southern Commission on the Study of Lynching that reported, "Sherman had felt the onset of the Depression more keenly than representative communities of similar size in Texas."[510]

Among those trying to "make it" in the county was George

Hughes, described in all media reports as "a forty-one-year-old Negro farm laborer" who was arrested on May 3, 1930 for the criminal sexual assault of a white woman. Hughes offered a coerced confession in the case involving the wife of his employer, but initially resisted arrest. Black residents of the community believed Hughes was falsely accused because his employer could not pay him six dollars in back wages owed and the rape accusation was trumped up to avoid paying him.

Arrested and housed at the Grayson County Courthouse jail, news quickly spread among the community's white residents alleging Hughes had not only raped an innocent, married white woman but had mutilated the woman's throat and breasts. Tensions ran high even before a trial could be conducted, with literally thousands of locals filling nearly every empty space on the courthouse square on May 9, 1930, demanding "justice."

As attorneys from both the state and the defense met with District Judge R. M. Carter and attempted to determine whether the case should go forward in Grayson County, or be moved to a community less enraged, trouble continued to boil outside the courthouse.

"Three times the mob unsuccessfully rushed the [courthouse] building," reporters noted, but were unsuccessful. On a fourth attempt, however, teenage boys were witnessed, "hurling a ten-gallon tank of gasoline through a basement window of the courthouse, and lighting it."[511]

Although firefighters were immediately summoned, their efforts to strike the fire were continuously thwarted by mob members cutting the fire hoses.[512]

"Aside from pushing the mob back by physical exertion and using their guns as clubs, tear bombs and water from fire hoses were the only methods employed by the officers in combatting the crowd," the Associated Press reported. "The mob became unruly shortly after Hughes was brought into the courtroom for trial. Officers were forced to use the [tear gas] bombs."[513]

As the courthouse fire raged, downtown businesses on the north side of the square were threatened by the growing inferno since little or no water was available to fight the fire due to the cut hoses. By nightfall, "the blackened walls of the courthouse were all that remained of the structure."[514]

Sheriff Arthur Vaughan, in attempt to disperse the crowd, repeatedly told rioters that Hughes likely had died in the fire after having been placed in the secured vault of the courthouse and away from the crowd outside. As the fire raged and ladders were placed against the courthouse to allow those trapped in the second floor courtroom to exit, the sheriff decided to move Hughes to a "fireproof" vault in the county clerk's office for his safety.

The sheriff told reporters "the Negro was given his choice of running to escape the mob, after the courthouse fire began, or of being shut in the vault. He chose the vault. When last seen by the officers, he was sitting in a chair in the vault, his head bowed upon his folded arms."[515]

Given a bucket of water and abandoned to the vault, Hughes died of smoke inhalation, but the mob was not satisfied.

"Members of the crowd waited until the flames subsided, then started pulling the blackened [courthouse] walls down in an attempt to cool off the vault" where they believed Hughes had survived. The vault was provided ventilation and an acetylene torch and a stick of dynamite were used to open the secured vault that remained intact amidst the ruins.[516]

Hughes was indeed found dead in the vault, but the rioters were not satiated. They dragged the dead man's body from the site and down the street to the "Negro business district" where he was hung from a cottonwood tree. Hughes' body remained dangling from the tree for a full day until it was finally cut down by National Guard troops dispatched to the city. The coroner ruled Hughes died of smoke inhalation, and his body was burned and hung post-mortem.

Eventually, as many as 400 National Guardsmen and Texas Rangers restored order in the town—but only after significant violence and arson had gutted not only the courthouse, but also much of the city's black business district.

"Guardsmen still were stationed at the corners of the courthouse square with machine guns, and were patrolling the streets of the town," national news wires reported more than a day after the riots. "Quiet prevailed in the city all day Sunday, the troopers' greatest difficulty being in directing traffic of swarming thousands of Sunday motorists drawn by curiosity to see the ruined courthouse and the Negro residence district stormed by the mob."[517]

The Texas National Guard took control of the city under a declaration of martial law made by Governor Dan Moody. Colonel Lawrence McGee declared, "We will stay here until we arrest as many of the mob members as possible, particularly leaders, and until the investigation is completed."[518]

Sherman's Mayor, Jess Eubanks, led the chorus of locals pinning blame for the violence on people from outside Sherman.

While condemning the rioting, Governor Moody prefaced his official statement on the ugly events at Sherman with an attempt at context. "The crime with which the Negro who was the object of the mob's fury was charged, was a brutal and atrocious thing and for it the death penalty awaited him," Governor Moody said. "The intimidation by the action of the mob that he would not have been speedily tried and legally executed is slander and libel on the good citizens of Grayson County."[519]

The tragedy at Sherman was statewide and national news. *The Kerrville Times*, a newspaper based more than 300 miles south of Sherman, editorialized that the lynching was prompted in part by "trumped up" defenses attorneys use to excuse deplorable behavior by their clients.

"The court delays and the technicalities resorted to by shrewd and unprincipled lawyers are indirectly the cause of many a community taking the law into its own hand," the editorial summarized. "The courts often get out of the hands of the good citizenship and are administered according to the wishes of shrewd criminal lawyers or the whims of sentimentalists who shed crocodile tears about any criminal that is brought to trial."[520]

Acknowledging that "any lynching is wrong" and that the events in Sherman "had some very shocking features" *The Kerrville Times* editors declared, "We must go deeper into the matter than surface indications and lay the blame where it belongs."[521]

Eventually, a Grayson County grand jury returned indictments against more than two dozen men for the riot and charged some police officers for complicity, although convictions were difficult to obtain amidst rumors, lies and poorly shielded efforts to protect the accused.[522] Actual indictments for burning the courthouse were never returned, although arson charges were leveled for burning businesses in the "Negro district."[523]

While the bulk of the charges brought were violations of Texas state law, four men were charged with federal offenses for attacks on National Guardsmen, including attempts to disarm them.[524]

The courthouse, a two-story structure featuring a cupola tower holding a clock and bell, was a total loss, estimated to be worth more than $100,000. With the arrival of the Great Depression, Grayson County went six years until a new courthouse was finally built, made possible in part with federal Works Progress Administration grants.[525]

A Hospital Patient is Lynched

WICOMICO COUNTY COURTHOUSE

December 4, 1931—Salisbury, Maryland

Local residents and historians have debated for decades the reason for an ugly turn of mob violence in the Eastern Shore community of Salisbury, Maryland, but the outcome has remained the same—a stain of "vigilante justice" has remained on the Wicomico County Courthouse.

In December 1931, the Depression was starting to take hold in communities big and small across the nation, including Salisbury, the economic center of the Delmarva Peninsula. The peninsula, a 170-mile long stretch bordered by the Chesapeake Bay, the Delaware River and the Atlantic Ocean, has a long history of contributing to the economies of the Eastern Shore of Maryland, Virginia and Delaware.

A community of just 10,000 residents, the D. J. Elliott & Son Company on Lake Street was one of the city's major business interests, employing as many as sixty men at one time. Operated by Daniel J. Elliott and his son James, the company was well known for quality baskets, wooden crates and other containers that were shipped across the world. The Elliott's also operated a wood mill that supplied lumber to builders across the region.

Although successful, the company would grow and shrink as orders and business would ebb and flow. Workers were paid about ten cents per hour in the 1930s for an eight-hour day. With jobs scarce and wages for what jobs existed in the nation stagnated, ideas about the benefits organized labor were easily capturing the attention of local workers.

As was usually the case, local business leaders such as D. J. Elliott and others, dismissed labor efforts as actually a front for Communist political interests. In Wicomico County, the International Labor Defense League was the prominent group organizing workers, a legal advocacy group gaining popularity among African-Americans for its strong stand against lynching and other acts of institutional racism.

Negro sources who talked to *The Baltimore Sun* (but would not give their name), said the labor organizers had been hoping to organize members based on the idea that "white employers were oppressing the Negroes on the Eastern Shore, defrauding them of their just wages and directly responsible for their unemployment."[526]

One of the workers the Labor Defense League had reached was twenty-three-year-old Matthew Williams, a laborer at the Elliott company earning about eight cents an hour. Williams, "who was reported on the borderline between low-grade intelligence and subnormality," had listened to speeches in the area given by representatives of the International Labor Defense League.

"Some persons have told authorities that they saw [Williams] pacing up and down in front of Mr. Elliott's factory on Lake Street for nearly an hour," just after eleven a.m. on Friday, December 4, 1931. Without warning, Williams entered the plant and went to Daniel Elliott's office and demanded a raise. Thwarted in his efforts, police determined Williams summarily shot Elliott in the head, and then shot himself.[527]

Williams was an employee of the Elliott company for nearly a decade and a "is said to have repeated remarks attributed to a Communist organizer and is reported to have asserted that if he ever killed a man, he would shoot himself," *The Baltimore Sun* reported.[528]

Severely wounded from his self-inflicted gunshot wound, Williams was immediately transported to the Peninsula General Hospital. Daniel Elliott, meanwhile, was pronounced dead at the scene.

The murder of a prominent white citizen by a reportedly "simple-minded" black man was an insidious event for many in Maryland, a state that has always had divided loyalties between progressive northern forces, and more conservative southern voices. As Clarence Mitchell, a Maryland civil rights leader noted, "Socially and economically, [Maryland's Eastern Shore] was closer to the South than the rest of Maryland, particularly in terms of race relations. . . . By the 1930s, the increased economic hardships of the Great Depression caused simmering hostilities to boil over, with violent result."[529]

While tensions remained, the matter seemed resolved when *The Daily Times*, the local newspaper in Salisbury, posted an update on the case on its front window reporting that

Williams had succumbed to his self-inflicted wounds. Within hours, however, the mood would change when the editors at *The Daily Times* updated their earlier report, and relayed news that Williams was still alive in the "colored" or "Negro ward" of the hospital.

The strange and ugly phenomenon of a mob quickly began to form, with as many as 300 men demanding that something be done to punish Williams immediately for his act of murder.

It wasn't long before the mob entered the Peninsula General Hospital (just before eight p.m.) where Williams was being treated for gunshot wounds to his shoulder and leg, and was confined to his hospital bed via the use of a straightjacket. The men in the mob "lifted him from his bed and ordered him to walk with them to the street. There more than 300 waiting men and women surrounded the Negro and walked him to the courthouse green at Main and Division street, three blocks distant," a detailed account in *The Baltimore Sun* indicated.[530]

The mob met little resistance from the hospital superintendent Helen V. Wise who was quoted as saying, "If you must take him, do it quietly."[531]

The Baltimore Sun reported, "The crowd, all men, which went to the hospital to get the Negro, was very orderly, the police here say. It was so quiet that they knew nothing of the pending action until someone stepped into the fire engine house on the way to the hospital to get a rope. By the time the additional members of the force arrived, the police chief and the deputy had been outmaneuvered and the Negro had been dropped out of the first-floor [hospital] window of the colored ward to the waiting mob."[532]

A rope was "flung over the limb of a tree, about twenty-five feet from the ground, and two others tied one end of it around the bandaged-swathed neck of the Negro. The men holding the rope tugged the Negro about fifteen feet about the ground as the mob, which had grown to about 2,000, applauded. The Negro was raised and lowered several times as the mob's shouts rose and fell. Finally, the rope was secured and Williams left hanging in the green. He was suspended in the green for about twenty minutes as the mob, constantly swelling, looked on. Then several men stepped forward, slashed the rope, and picked up the Negro's body, shouting to the mob to follow them."[533]

Wicomico County Sheriff G. Murray Phillips attempted to get the mob to let the body go once the deed was done, "but was brushed aside by the mob, which had started to close in. They dragged the body to a lot on Poplar Hill Avenue, within easy view of scores of Negro homes, and after drenching it with gasoline, set it afire. . . . new recruits [to the mob] grouped about the pyre. They did not disperse until the last flame flickered out."[534]

A more detailed account of the ugly scene came from the Crusader News Agency indicating that members of the mob cut off the fingers and toes from Williams' body and "threw them on the porches and in the yards of the colored people's homes, shouting that the 'Niggers can make a sandwich out of them.' They then threw the gasoline over him, set a match to him and while the human torch burned, they passed booze around, drinking and singing."[535]

Interestingly, the local newspaper in Salisbury, *The Daily Times* seemed subdued in its coverage of the lynching, printing only an eleven-paragraph account under a small headline.

The newspaper did issue a front page "statement" in which they explained they would "omit the details of the demonstration here last night when Matthew Williams, confessed slayer of D. J. Elliott, was hanged in the Courthouse square for the very obvious reason that almost every reader of our paper has had an opportunity to learn of them first hand from eyewitnesses. The facts which formed the background for the demonstration . . . are well known and a repetition of them would be superfluous. The slaying of Mr. Elliott was deplorable as was also the mob scene. . . . We at all times deplore violence, either of an individual or a congregation of individuals, but when violence is done, it behooves every one of us to cooperate in speeding up a return to absolutely normal and harmonious conditions."[536]

What coverage *The Daily Times* did provide the scene playing out practically outside the front door of its offices focused on the coroner's investigation into Williams' death. The report also attempted to shift blame for the dreadful spectacle onto people from outside of Salisbury, noting, "The opinion prevails that many of those participating in the actual hanging came from other sections of the peninsula and that their actions were prompted by events that have occurred in their own communities."[537]

Maryland Governor Cabell Ritchie was out of the state at a meeting in New York, but had been informed of the events in Salisbury. Ritchie offered what is best described as a rambling, meaningless "statement" via a telegraph cable: "I will leave New York on the Midnight train for Baltimore. . . . I want to ascertain the exact facts in reference to this case before making any statement. If they are as reported briefly to me tonight, I will have something to say, and something very emphatic to say."[538]

Louis J. O'Donnell, a correspondent *The Baltimore Sun* dispatched to Salisbury to cover the story, reported that the day after the lynching, "Only two or three of Salisbury's Negro population of 1,500 appeared on the principal streets of the town tonight. Their scarcity was the result of efforts made during the day with the cooperation of Negro leaders to curtail their customary Saturday night influx of Negroes as a precaution against racial reaction to the lynching. . . . Of the citizens here who would volunteer opinions on the case, few voiced any regret for the Negro who killed his employer."[539]

State's Attorney Levin C. Bailey assured Wicomico County residents, "There will be no more delay than is necessary for the identification of those who took part in this crime. I plan to prosecute this case vigorously, stopping not at the leaders, but carrying it to every other person who took part who can be identified."[540]

Despite the pledges of a thorough investigation, the outcome was predictable feckless. In March 1932, a grand jury heard testimony from 124 witnesses regarding the lynching, but reported they lacked sufficient evidence to indict anyone for the murder of Matthew Williams.

The official grand jury reported stated, "After a thoroughly energetic and complete investigation of all the evidence, direct and indirect, rumors and every lead indicated by the evidence given by more than one-hundred witnesses . . . we find that there is absolutely no evidence that can remotely connect anyone with the instigation or perpetration of the murder of Mathew [sic.] Williams."[541] The grand jury also dismissed the idea that a Communist organization was in place in the county.

The Baltimore Sun reported, "While residents of the town have evinced a keen interest in the progress of the investigation, little surprise was expressed as a result."[542]

The Law Saves a Suspect, but not the Courthouse

BEDFORD COUNTY COURTHOUSE

December 19, 1934—Shelbyville, Tennessee

The determined efforts of a Bedford County judge and members of the Tennessee National Guard saved a black man from lynching at the courthouse in Shelbyville, but could not save the courthouse itself.

On December 19, 1934, a trial was attempted inside the courthouse for E. K. Harris, a twenty-two-year-old "Negro suspect" accused of "criminally assaulting" a fourteen-year-old white girl. Harris had been held since his November 19 arrest on the charge.

The trial never could proceed, however, as rioters outside the courthouse seeking to lynch Harris succeeding in setting the courthouse on fire. The fire eventually destroyed the courthouse originally opened in 1872.

State and local officials tried diligently to keep peace and order, with Tennessee Governor Hill McAlister dispatching 500 of the state's National Guard troops to Shelbyville, a community about 60 miles southeast of Nashville, to reinforce the 100 troops already in place.

By mid-afternoon, despite repeated attempts to restore order, several fires were started by rioters in the lower level offices of the courthouse. By 7:30 p.m., with the help of "gasoline bombs" hurled through basement windows of the courthouse, the edifice was awash in flames.

The angry mob had grown angrier in the day when they learned Harris was successfully smuggled away from the city camouflaged in a National Guard uniform.

"Immediately after the Negro, disguised in clothing of the National Guard and his face covered with a gas mask to shield his color, was hurriedly locked in a cell, all doors to the jail were closed and locked to visitors. . . . the Negro prisoner was forced to lie flat on the floor in the back of the car on the fast trip [to Nashville]," *The Nashville Tennessean* reported. "The party arrived [at Nashville] at 4:07 o'clock a little more than an hour after they had sped out of Shelbyville with the cries of the mob ringing in their ears."[543]

Judge T. L. Coleman said the attack by the mob was "very regrettable and deplorable" and worth a criminal investigation of its own. "The adjutant general told me that he could handle the situation so as to have the trial, but that it might result in the killing of as many of 100 people," Judge Coleman said. "I told him I didn't want that done and that I would declare a mistrial to avoid bloodshed."[544]

Beyond the spectacular blaze that leveled the courthouse (and threatened an entire block of businesses across the street from the courthouse square), three men were killed and several others wounded.

Among the dead, Dr. James L. Morton, the county health officer, said one unidentified body was brought to the front porch of the hospital at 3:30 p.m., but then was taken away moments later "by unknown persons and without attendants at the hospital having had an opportunity to learn his name." The man was described as twenty-five years old. Morton said a total of nineteen persons were treated for injuries, one of them critically injured. Wounds suffered were mostly gunshot or buckshot wounds.[545]

Morton identified one of the dead men as R. E. Edwards, forty-two years old, a house painter from Shelbyville, believed involved in the protest. Two others died later including Floyd "Pat" Lawes, twenty-eight, a Shelbyville firefighter called to help quell the scene, and Gilford Freeman, a local machinist (also allegedly involved in the mob). All three men suffered gunshot wounds. Lawes was identified as a relative of the young girl who reported the assault.

The courthouse was considered a total loss, flames ripping through the roof causing the ornate bell tower copula to collapse. "The building was reduced to a hull of charred walls . . . The flames started in the office of Sheriff T. E. Gant, where a large quantity of gasoline had been poured by a group of men who had forewarned the city fire department that the building would be destroyed to express their resentment of the matter in which Sheriff Gant had handled the Negro's case. They were especially enraged because guardsmen had been brought here to keep order during the trial."[546]

At first there was hope that the fire would not be large, with flames dying down at one point, but "later members of the fire department discovered flames breaking through the ceiling of the first floor. The blaze gained headway rapidly, and soon the structure was a mass of flames."

Eyewitnesses reported that firefighters were thwarted in their efforts by members of the mob, some of them attacking the firefighters and others using axes to cut water hoses rolled out to fight the blaze. "Water was turned off a number of times as firemen sought vainly to put out the flames," one newspaper account told.[547]

"The mob ceased its destruction temporarily when it looked as if the entire northwest side of the [courthouse] square would be on fire and turned to aid in checking the flames," *The Nashville Tennessean* reported.[548]

Sheriff's deputies said they believed dynamite thrown through a south window of the courthouse exploded in the fire, "sending a balloon of fire and smoke three hundred feet in the air" and "heat from the terrific explosion was felt a block away."[549]

Roof fires on some downtown buildings did erupt with embers carried by wind from the courthouse fire, but were extinguished and private stores and buildings were saved.

After Harris was secreted away from Shelbyville by National Guard troops, the mob turned its anger on four National Guard trucks left unattended. The trucks were reportedly flipped and burned by the mob, including their machine guns and equipment.

In all, three separate attacks were repelled as Judge Coleman attempted to hold court, once with tear gas—but when troops stepped inside the courthouse for fear of fire from possible snipers, the final mob push came.

"The third attack came at 2:45 p.m., the guardsmen took their stand in the hall of the courthouse. . . . Firing against the floor, the troops effected a ricocheting of bullets that splattered the legs and ankles of the crowd. In the final attack of the crowd stormed the courthouse, battered down the door and rushed into the main hallway."

As the mob broke through, "It was then that the troops opened up on the crowd with .45 automatic pistols and riot guns. The crowd had reached the porch of the courthouse without a move from the guardsmen. One man, in the forefront, seized a bench on the porch and crashed it through the glass of the front door. The guardsmen then opened fire."[550]

Bedford County Circuit Court Clerk W. A. Landers said he was able to save some of the county's records in his office before the evening fire worsened, but most were destroyed.

Regular excuses could be found in the aftermath, some locals wanting to blame "out of towners" for the violence. Others noted that a great amount of drinking had taken place during the day—a cold day with light snow flurries and a twenty-mile northwest wind "which cut like a knife was held responsible for much of the drinking."[551]

While further violence was avoided, the shadow of the downtown riot hung over the city as the smoldering remains of the courthouse smoked for days.

"The holiday spirit was dampened here today by fears of mob violence," an Associated Press dispatch indicated. "Many felt that today, bringing hundreds of Christmas shoppers to swell the usual holiday crowd, would see a crisis in the tense situation that has existed since rioting Wednesday."[552]

The suspect in the case, young Harris was eventually tried on the original assault charge in Nashville, and was convicted and sentenced to be executed for his crime. The Tennessee Supreme Court affirmed the ruling in the Harris sentence.[553]

Two years after the mob attack meant to take his life, reporters took note that E. K. Harris was dead anyway. "Saved from a mob whose clashes with National Guardsmen caused four deaths . . . was electrocuted Friday for an attack on a young white girl."[554]

The AP reported that Harris "entered the [electric] chair, grinning foolishly, his stomach filled with fried chicken, and was worried only about the disposition of his body. He didn't want it cut up my medical students, and prison officials assured him that his mother had arranged to claim the body, and take it back to Shelbyville for burial."[555]

Prison Warden A. W. Neely said Harris continued to maintain his innocence until shortly before the execution when he reportedly made "a full confession."[556] Neely said the confession came after Harris "got religion" and was baptized in the prison pool "by an aged Negro preacher doing two years for murder. At the baptizing yesterday, the prison Negro sang spirituals with other prisoners who gathered 'round."[557]

On January 7, 1935, a committee was appointed by county officials to begin planning for a new courthouse, while temporary quarters were located for county courts and offices displaced in the riot-induced fire.[558] In May 1935, a bond issue of $170,000 was sold to fund building a new courthouse.[559] The new courthouse was completed and reopened in 1936.

"The Last Classic Lynching in America"

PEARL RIVER COUNTY COURTHOUSE

April-May 1959—Poplarville, Mississippi

In 1937, writer and poet Abel Meeropol (writing under the name Lewis Allan) published a poem called "Strange Fruit" as a protest against the culture of lynching that permeated many parts of the United States.

The poem, later recorded into a famous song by blues vocalist Billie Holliday, declared "Southern trees bear a strange fruit, blood on the leaves and blood at the root, black bodies swinging in the Southern breeze, strange fruit hanging from the poplar trees."[560]

Poplar trees grow like weeds in Pearl River County in southern Mississippi, and influenced the naming of the county seat Poplarville. Ironically, Poplarville is known as the site of "one of the last classic lynchings" of a black man in America—one of more than 1,900 recorded in US history.[561]

Just after Midnight on April 25, 1959, an angry mob entered (virtually without resistance) the historic Pearl River County Courthouse in downtown Poplarville and removed twenty-two-year-old Mack Charles Parker from a second floor jail cell. Parker was being held on a charge related to a sexual assault.

"Hooded night raiders, gloved against fingerprints, dragged a screaming Negro charged with assaulting a white woman from his jail cell today, leaving few clues for converging FBI agents," the Associated Press reported.[562]

The AP dispatch reflected the change slowly coming related to issues of "southern justice happening at the dawn of the nation's Civil Rights movement. Immediately the attention of the Federal Bureau of Investigation and Director J. Edgar Hoover turned to the matter. Hoover ordered agents from the New Orleans field office—just seventy miles southwest of Poplarville—to converge on the small community of just 2,000 residents to assist in the investigation.

The AP reported that "local deputies, state highway patrolmen and volunteers ranged through the red clay hills of Pearl River County" for Parker, "but found nothing."[563]

While family members held out hope that Parker somehow had survived the human rampage, Pearl County Sheriff W. O. Moody openly expressed doubt that the young man was still alive. Moody confirmed that the courthouse jail had no guard on duty during the overnight hours, with inmates simply locked inside.

"Only bloodstains haphazardly scattered around the second floor [courthouse jail] cell, down the stairs, and along a tiled corridor indicated the path along which the hooded raiders had dragged Parker into the night," an AP dispatch detailed.[564]

One witness to the abduction—and presumed lynching—was fellow inmate C. J. Mondy who told the sheriff "his captors dragged Parker out of the building by his heels, his head thumping on the steel treads of the [courthouse] stairs. When they dumped Parker into the getaway car, the Negro screamed and howled and renewed his struggle. The car roared away."[565]

Mondy said the gang of nine or ten men wore stockings over their faces and beat Parker with a broom handle and metal garbage can lid. "Parker kept shouting for help," Mondy said. "Once a member of the mob asked him, 'Why did you do it?' and Parker cried that he did not do it and tried to blame other inmates in the jail."[566]

Officials in adjacent Forrest County were particularly interested in the abduction of Parker as his accuser, a twenty-four-year-old white woman and her family lived there. The woman had picked Parker out of a line-up as the man who had approached her broken down car in a rural area and raped her in front of her five-year-old child (while her husband was gone looking for help to get their car started).

The day after Parker's abduction, sixteen FBI agents set up shop inside a courtroom in the Pearl River County Courthouse to interview all of the inmates present at the time of the crime.

FBI agents also questioned John Reyer, a local farmer, who was exiting the Pearl River County Hospital across the street from the courthouse as the men were leaving with Parker, screaming for help. "I'm afraid I couldn't help that fellow much," Reyer told reporters. "All I know is that it was a four-door car, I saw them throw him in the back of the car and then jumped into the car and took off fast. They drove east on the road, but I didn't see where they went after that."[567]

Mississippi Governor J. P. Coleman, a former district attorney, judge and state attorney general (although an avowed segregationist), pledged the state's full support in finding the culprits of the crime. Coleman said the crime "comes at a bad time" and that "People in Mississippi as a whole don't approve of this sort of thing. We hope the vast majorities of Mississippians won't be punished by civil rights legislation for what a handful of men have done in violating the law."[568]

More than a week passed and little news emerged about where Parker was—or where his body was. As *The Jackson Clarion-Ledger* reported, "Life went on much as usual in Poplarville on Sunday as officers pushed the hunt for Mack Charles Parker, the Negro taken from the Pearl River County Courthouse Jail. . . . [however] later in the day streets were crowded with cars and townspeople who drove and walked around the jail."[569]

On Monday morning, Circuit Court Judge Sebe Dale held a hearing to officially determine that Parker's trial on the charges of rape could not go forward because "the floodgates of hate and hell" had been opened up on the people of Mississippi. "The people [of Mississippi] have been sinned against. They do not deserve it."[570]

District Attorney William Stewart officially asked for a continuation of the case "because we have no defendant" present.[571]

"A fair trial has been denied this man," Judge Dale declared, perhaps knowing that the man was likely already dead. "I believe had he been tried, the record would have brought a kinder feeling toward the people of Mississippi."[572]

Turning his remarks to the growing fear among many of the state's leaders about pending civil rights legislation, Judge Dale weighed in by saying "I do not know what to expect, what laws will be passed against us."[573]

Stewart openly discussed theories that the FBI was exploring whether the abduction of Parker from the courthouse jail had been an "inside job" since it was carried out with such efficiency, and no resistance. Sheriff Moody, however, said that the layout and operations of the county jail were well known to most everyone.

Fears that FBI assistance in the investigation would be withdrawn were tamped down in the days that followed when the White House released the contents of a telegram from President Dwight D. Eisenhower to Governor Coleman confirming that federal help would remain as long as needed. Eisenhower's telegram said it was "his earnest hope that there will be swift apprehension of the guilty persons."[574]

Finally, on Monday, May 4, 1959, part of a posse of sixty FBI agents and Mississippi highway patrolmen pulled a badly decomposed body from the Pearl River near Bogalusa, Louisiana, about twenty miles west of Poplarville.

Although no bullets were found in the body—later confirmed to be that of Parker—it was determined he had been shot twice in the chest and the side. Just hours after a coroner's inquest was completed into the death, "about 100 Negroes attended funeral services for Parker in a cemetery about one mile from his home outside Lumberton, Mississippi."[575]

Rev. W. M. Watkins told the mourners, "We cannot tell where his soul is until Judgment Day, but all of us must continue to love our neighbors, no matter what has occurred."[576]

Another minister, Rev. Nelson Wheeler prayed, "I pray God, you will have mercy on everyone; won't you help us to be a stronger people; to give us power to love everybody?"[577]

Parker's casket was draped in an American flag reflecting his status as a US Army veteran. At the time of his death, he was working as an over-the-road truck driver.

Police and prosecutors told reporters their rape case against Parker was sound and likely would have resulted in a conviction, but there were doubters in the community, especially among black citizens.

Parker's mother Eliza talked to a black newspaper reporter from Baltimore asking "Why" Oh, Lord, why?" through her tears. She relayed "I tried to get him a white lawyer, but I couldn't. No one would take the case."[578]

Once she did obtain a lawyer, a local black attorney named R. Jess Brown, she said she shared her concerns for her son's safety at the jail. "I went to see my boy at the courthouse Monday just to talk to him. I said, 'Son, did you do this?' and he said, 'No, ma'am. I didn't do it. I did not do it.'"[579]

Mrs. Parker asked aloud, "Couldn't they give him a trial? If he had been given a fair trial and they proved it, and he went to the electric chair, I could at least know it happened because he was guilty. Even if he did it, he was entitled to a fair trial."[580]

His accuser, a young woman from Pearl, Mississippi, spoke anonymously to reporters and said, "I don't know who lynched him, but it was wrong" and added, "It's terrible that a lynch mob kidnapped him, I'd prefer that he had a trial." She reaffirmed that Parker "looked like" the man who had assaulted her.[581]

As a report in *The Afro-American* newspaper in Baltimore, Maryland indicated that the young woman "showed little remorse or sadness" while admitting she "wasn't certain" Parker was her attacker, even though she had identified him.[582]

"When I saw his picture in the newspaper the next day, it looked just like the man on the road that night"—referring to the February 25, 1959 assault that led to Parker's arrest.[583]

The accuser, originally from Watertown, New York, had relocated to Mississippi and was married to a plumbing supply salesman. She directly addressed rumors that she had made up the story about a rape to cover an extra-marital affair she had engaged.

"Rumors went around that I was made pregnant by this colored man," she said. "But it's a lie."[584]

She also denied rumors that family and friends of her had led the lynching to help her avoid the embarrassment of a rape trial. "I wouldn't have minded [a trial]," she said. "I would have gone right through with it. That's the right way."[585]

At thc timc of Parker's lynching death, Mississippi led the nation with the most such cases since records were kept. Parker's was the 579th such death recorded in Mississippi state history.[586]

In 2009, Parker's death was among a series of cases to be reopened by the FBI under a cold-case effort to clear civil rights-related deaths. Despite the effort, however, no arrests were ever made in Parker's death.

ACKNOWLEDGEMENTS

ABOUT THE AUTHOR

ANDREW E. STONER is a professor of Communication Studies at California State University, Sacramento. A native of Indiana, he is the author of a variety of non-fiction works, including biographies and true crime texts. He holds a PhD in Public Communication and Technology from Colorado State University, a master's degree in journalism from Ball State University, and a bachelor's degree in journalism from Franklin College of Indiana. He has worked as both a newspaper reporter, and a communications expert in the public and private sector.

ENDNOTES

x McDevitt, Ray. 2001. *Courthouses of California: An Illustrated History*. San Francisco, California. California Historical Society.

1 Chicago Tribune, Jan. 12, 1937; Wojcik, Russell (2013, December 13). *A History: Courthouse Place*. Published online at: http://newmanknowschicago.com/a-history-courthouse-place/. Retrieved June 17, 2017.

2 United Press International, July 21, 1924

3 Associated Press, July 21, 1924

4 Ibid.

5 United Press International, July 21, 1924

6 Associated Press, July 21, 1924

7 Ibid.

8 Ibid.

9 Ibid.

10 Ibid.

11 Ibid.

12 Ibid.

13 Chicago Tribune, July 22, 1924

14 Ibid.

15 Associated Press, July 21, 1924

16 Ibid.

17 Chicago Tribune, July 28, 1924

18 Chicago Tribune, Aug. 12, 1924

19 Associated Press, July 24, 1924

20 Chicago Tribune, July 25, 1924

21 Ibid.

22 Chicago Tribune, July 24, 1924

23 Chicago Tribune, July 27, 1924

24 Ibid.

25 Chicago Tribune, Sept. 9, 1924

26 Ibid.

27 Chicago Tribune, Sept. 10, 1924

28 Ibid.

29 Chicago Tribune, Sept. 9, 1924
30 Ibid.
31 Chicago Tribune, Sept. 11, 1924
32 Chicago Tribune, Feb. 19, 1936
33 Ibid.
34 Ibid.
35 Ibid.
36 Chicago Tribune, July 29, 1957
37 Ibid.
38 Ibid.
39 Ibid.
40 Chicago Tribune, March 6, 1958
41 Van West, Carroll. (1998). *The Tennessee Encyclopedia of History & Culture*. Nashville, Tenn.: Tennessee Historical Society.
42 Associated Press, July 9, 1925
43 Olson, Steven P. (2003). *The Trial of John T. Scopes: A Primary Source Account*. New York: Rosen Publishing Group.
44 Chattanooga Daily News, May 4, 1925
45 Olson, Steven P. (2003). *The Trial of John T. Scopes: A Primary Source Account*. New York: Rosen Publishing Group.
46 Associated Press, July 6, 1925
47 Ibid.
48 Ibid.
49 Chicago Tribune, July 10, 1925
50 Associated Press, July 6, 1925
51 Nashville Tennessean, July 7, 1925
52 Associated Press, July 9, 1925
53 Ibid.
54 Ibid.
55 Associated Press, July 10, 1925
56 Chillicothe (MO) Constitution-Tribune, July 10, 1925
57 Associated Press, July 11, 1925
58 Ibid.
59 Associated Press, July 13, 1925
60 Chicago Tribune, July 10, 1925
61 Associated Press, July 13, 1925
62 Chicago Tribune, July 10, 1925
63 Chillicothe (MO) Constitution-Tribune, July 10, 1925
64 Ibid.
65 Associated Press, July 17, 1925
66 Indianapolis News, July 21, 1925
67 St. Louis Post-Dispatch, July 21, 1925
68 Ibid.
69 Ibid.

70 Ibid.
71 Los Angeles Times, July 21, 1925
72 Ibid.
73 Los Angeles Times, July 21, 1925=
74 St. Louis Post-Dispatch, July 21, 1925
75 Indiana Historical Society, Indianapolis, Ind.
76 Moore, Leonard J. (1997). *Citizen Klansman: The Ku Klux Klan in Indiana, 1921-1928*. Chapel Hill, NC: University of North Carolina Press.
77 Ibid.
78 Indianapolis Star, Nov. 15, 1925
79 Ibid.=
80 Ibid.
81 Indianapolis News, July 7, 1925
82 Indianapolis Star, Oct. 29, 1925
83 Indianapolis Star, Nov. 15, 1925
84 Muncie Evening Press, Oct. 29, 1925
85 Ibid.
86 Ibid.
87 Ibid.
88 Indianapolis News, Nov. 14, 1925
89 Muncie Evening Press, Oct. 29, 1925
90 Muncie Star-Press, Nov. 14, 1925
91 Ibid.
92 Indianapolis Star, Nov. 16, 1925
93 Associated Press, Nov. 14, 1925
94 Ibid.
95 Indianapolis Star, Nov. 15, 1925
96 Indianapolis News, Nov. 14, 1925
97 Indianapolis Star, Nov. 15, 1925
98 Ibid.
99 Ibid.
100 Ibid.
101 Ibid.
102 Indianapolis News, Nov. 17, 1925
103 Ibid.
104 Ibid.
105 Associated Press, Nov. 19, 1925
106 Indianapolis Star, July 30, 1927
107 Indianapolis News, July 30, 1927
108 Ibid.
109 Indianapolis Star, July 30, 1927
110 Scripps-Howard News Service, Oct. 18, 1954
111 Associated Press, Oct. 17, 1954

112 Cleveland Plain-Dealer, July 5, 1954; Akron (OH) Beacon-Journal, July 6, 1954
113 Akron (OH) Beacon-Journal, July 6, 1954
114 Ibid.
115 St. Louis Post-Dispatch, Oct. 18, 1954
116 Associated Press, Dec. 22, 1954
117 Neal, James. (2001). *The Wrong Man: The Final Verdict on the Dr. Sam Sheppard Murder Case.* New York: Random House.
118 Scripps-Howard News Service, Oct. 18, 1954
119 Akron (OH) Beacon-Journal, Oct. 17, 1954
120 Associated Press, Dec. 22, 1954
121 Associated Press, Dec. 1, 1954
122 Ibid.
123 Ibid.
124 Ibid.
125 Ibid.
126 Ibid.
127 Ibid.
128 Associated Press, Dec. 10, 1954
129 Ibid.
130 Ibid.
131 Ibid.
132 Ibid.
133 St. Louis Post-Dispatch, Oct. 18, 1954
134 Ibid.
135 International News Service, Dec. 7, 1954
136 Associated Press, Dec. 22, 1954
137 Ibid.
138 Ibid.
139 Neal, James. (2001). *The Wrong Man: The Final Verdict on the Dr. Sam Sheppard Murder Case.* New York: Random House.
140 Ibid.
141 Ibid.
142 Ibid.
143 Lawler, Jerry. (2002). *It's Good to Be the King... Sometimes.* New York: World Wrestling Entertainment.
144 Los Angeles Times, Aug. 2, 1957
145 Ibid.
146 Hofler, Robert. (2005). *The Man Who Invented Rock Hudson: The Pretty Boys and Dirty Deals of Henry Willson.* New York: Carroll & Graf Publishers.
147 Los Angeles Times, Aug. 2, 1957
148 Los Angeles Times, Aug. 8, 1957
149 Ibid.

150 United Press International, Aug. 6, 1957; Los Angeles Times, Aug. 8, 1957
151 Los Angeles Times, Aug. 8, 1957
152 United Press International, Aug. 7, 1957
153 Long Beach (CA) Independent, Aug. 14, 1957
154 Hollywood Reporter, Aug. 13, 2015
155 Hofler, Robert. (2005). *The Man Who Invented Rock Hudson: The Pretty Boys and Dirty Deals of Henry Willson.* New York: Carroll & Graf Publishers,
156 Associated Press, Aug. 1, 1957
157 Hofler, Robert. (2005). *The Man Who Invented Rock Hudson: The Pretty Boys and Dirty Deals of Henry Willson.* New York: Carroll & Graf Publishers.
158 Long Beach (CA) Independent, Aug. 15, 1957
159 Los Angeles Times, Aug. 15, 1957
160 Los Angeles Times, Aug. 15, 1957
161 Long Beach (CA) Independent, Aug. 15, 1957
162 Ibid.
163 Long Beach (CA) Independent, Aug. 15, 1957; Los Angeles Times, Aug. 15, 1957
164 Los Angeles Times, Aug. 15, 1957
165 Ibid.
166 Long Beach (CA) Independent, Aug. 15, 1957
167 Los Angeles Times, Aug. 15, 1957
168 Long Beach (CA) Independent, Aug. 15, 1957
169 Los Angeles Times, Aug. 15, 1957
170 Long Beach (CA) Independent, Aug. 15, 1957
171 Ibid.
172 Los Angeles Times, Aug. 8, 1957
173 Los Angeles Times, Aug. 14, 1957
174 Associated Press, Aug. 3, 1957
175 Ibid.
176 Long Beach (CA) Independent, Aug. 14, 1957
177 Ibid.
178 Long Beach (CA) Independent, Aug. 14, 1957; Los Angeles Times, Aug. 14, 1957
179 Los Angeles Times, Aug. 14, 1957
180 Long Beach (CA) Independent, Aug. 14, 1957
181 Associated Press, Aug. 17, 1957
182 Ibid.
183 Ibid.
184 Ibid.
185 Ibid.
186 Los Angeles Times, Aug. 17, 1957

187 Ibid.
188 Los Angeles Times, Aug. 31, 1957
189 Ibid.
190 Associated Press, Aug. 19, 1957
191 Los Angeles Times, Sept. 4, 1957
192 Ibid.
193 Ibid.
194 Ibid.
195 Ibid.
196 Los Angeles Times, Aug. 31, 1957
197 Associated Press, Aug. 19, 1957
198 Associated Press, Aug. 30, 1957
199 Museum of Broadcast Communications. Retrieved online at: http://www.museum.tv/eotv/kennedyjf.htm
200 Ibid.
201 Report of the President's Commission on the Assassination of President John F. Kennedy. (1964).

202 Hannan, Caryn. (2008). *Illinois Biographical Directory*. Hamburg, Mich.: State History Publications, LLC; *Valley Morning Star* (Harlingen, TX), Nov. 26, 1963

203 Cartwright, Gary. (1975, November). "Who was Jack Ruby?" *Texas Monthly* magazine.
204 Ibid.
205 *Valley Morning Star* (Harlingen, TX), Nov. 26, 1963
206 Summers, Anthony. (1998). *Not in Your Lifetime.* New York: Marlowe & Company.
207 Brown, Joe B. (2001). *Dallas and the Jack Ruby Trial: Memoir of Judge Joe B. Brown, Sr.* Diane Holloway, editor. Bloomington, Ind.: iUniverse Books.
208 Associated Press, Dec. 24, 1963
209 Brown, Joe B. (2001). *Dallas and the Jack Ruby Trial: Memoir of Judge Joe B. Brown, Sr.* Diane Holloway, editor. Bloomington, Ind.: iUniverse Books.
210 Ibid.
211 Associated Press, Dec. 24, 1963
212 Ibid.
213 Ibid.
214 Brown, Joe B. (2001). *Dallas and the Jack Ruby Trial: Memoir of Judge Joe B. Brown, Sr.* Diane Holloway, editor. Bloomington, Ind.: iUniverse Books.
215 Ibid.
216 Ibid.

217 Ibid.
218 United Press International, Feb. 21, 1964
219 Ibid.
220 *Kansas City Star*, Feb. 21, 1964
221 *El Paso Herald-Post*, March 7, 1964
222 Brown, Joe B. (2001). *Dallas and the Jack Ruby Trial: Memoir of Judge Joe B. Brown, Sr.* Diane Holloway, editor. Bloomington, Ind.: iUniverse Books.
223 *El Paso Herald-Post*, March 7, 1964
224 United Press International, March 14, 1964
225 Ibid.
226 *Chicago Tribune*, April 24, 1964
227 *Dallas Morning News*, Jan. 4, 1967; Associated Press, Jan. 4, 1967
228 *Dallas Morning News*, June 30, 2015
229 Life magazine, July 29, 1966
230 Ibid.
231 Ibid.
232 Ibid.
233 Mount Vernon (IL) Register-News, April 3, 1967
234 Life magazine, July 29, 1966
235 Bloomington (IL) Pantagraph, April 6, 1967
236 Ibid.
237 Ibid.
238 Ibid.
239 Ibid.
240 Ibid.
241 Ibid.
242 Chicago Tribune, Dec. 20, 1966
243 Chicago Tribune, Feb. 15, 1967
244 Ibid.
245 Mount Vernon (IL) Register-News, April 3, 1967
246 Chicago Tribune, April 5, 1967
247 Ibid.
248 Ibid.
249 Ibid.
250 Chicago Tribune, April 13, 1967; Bloomington (IL) Pantagraph, April 13, 1967
251 Chicago Tribune, April 18, 1967
252 Ibid.
253 Bloomington (IL) Pantagraph, April 19, 1967
254 United Press International, April 21, 1967
255 Associated Press, June 5, 1967
256 Chicago Tribune, June 6, 1967
257 Ibid.

258 Ibid.
259 Chicago Tribune, June 29, 1971
260 Chicago Tribune, Nov. 22, 1972
261 Greene, Bob. (1993). *Bob Greene American Beat*. New York: Sterling Publishing Company, Inc.
262 New York Times, May 16, 1996; Chicago Tribune, May 15, 1996
263 Chicago Tribune, April 25, 2016
264 Associated Press, Oct. 28, 2014
265 Ibid.
266 Associated Press, Nov. 20, 2017
267 Associated Press, July 24, 1970
268 Ibid.
269 Ibid.
270 Ibid.
271 Los Angeles Times, July 28, 1970
272 Associated Press, July 29, 1970
273 Ibid.
274 Ibid.
275 Ibid.
276 United Press International, July 30, 1970
277 Ibid.
278 Ibid.
279 Los Angeles Times, Aug. 4, 1970
280 Ibid.
281 Associated Press, Sept. 6, 1970; Los Angeles Downtown News, Oct. 10, 2014
282 Los Angeles Times, Oct. 2, 1970
283 Ibid.
284 Ibid.
285 Ibid.
286 Ibid.
287 Ibid.
288 Ibid.
289 Ibid.
290 Ibid.
291 Associated Press, Oct. 7, 1970
292 Ibid.
293 Ibid.
294 Los Angeles Times, Oct. 6, 1970
295 Ibid.
296 Los Angeles Times, Nov. 21, 1970
297 Ibid.
298 Ibid.
299 Atlanta magazine, March 4, 2013

300 Associated Press, March 3, 1978; New York Times, March 6, 1978
301 Houston Post, Aug. 11, 2012
302 New York Times, March 6, 1978
303 Akron (OH) Beacon-Journal, March 7, 1978
304 New York Times, March 6, 1978
305 Washington Post, March 7, 1978
306 United Press International, March 7, 1978
307 Ibid.
308 Akron (OH) Beacon-Journal, March 7, 1978
309 Associated Press, March 8, 1978
310 United Press International, March 7, 1978
311 Ibid.
312 Flynt, Larry, with Kenneth Ross. (1996). *An Unseemly Man: My Life as Pornographer, Pundit, and Social Outcast.* Beverly Hills, CA: Phoenix Books.
313 Atlanta magazine, March 4, 2013
314 Ibid.
315 Los Angeles Times, March 6, 1978
316 Associated Press, March 3, 1978
317 New York Daily News, March 7, 1978
318 Ibid.
319 Ibid.
320 Flynt, Larry, with Kenneth Ross. (1996). *An Unseemly Man: My Life as Pornographer, Pundit, and Social Outcast.* Beverly Hills, CA: Phoenix Books.
321 New York Times, March 6, 1978
322 Flynt, Larry, with Kenneth Ross. (1996). *An Unseemly Man: My Life as Pornographer, Pundit, and Social Outcast.* Beverly Hills, CA: Phoenix Books.
323 Ibid.
324 New York Times, March 6, 1978
325 Washington Post, March 7, 1978
326 Washington Star, June 6, 1978
327 Ibid.
328 Ibid.
329 Ibid.
330 Ibid.
331 Ibid.
332 St. Louis Post-Dispatch, Feb. 2, 1997
333 CNN, Nov. 20, 2013
334 St. Louis Post-Dispatch, Feb. 2, 1997
335 CNN, Nov. 20, 2013
336 St. Louis Post-Dispatch, Feb. 2, 1997
337 Atlanta magazine, March 4, 2013

338 Ibid.
339 Chicago Tribune, Feb. 7, 1980
340 Ibid.
341 Ibid.
342 Ibid.
343 Ibid.
344 Ibid.
345 Ibid.
346 Ibid.
347 Ibid.
348 Ibid.
349 Ibid.
350 Chicago Tribune, Feb. 8, 1980
351 Ibid.
352 Ibid.
353 Chicago Tribune, Feb. 9, 1980
354 Chicago Tribune, Feb. 26, 1980
355 Ibid.
356 Ibid.
357 Ibid.
358 Ibid.
359 Ibid.
360 Ibid.
361 Ibid.
362 Associated Press, March 8, 1980
363 Ibid.
364 Ibid.
365 Ibid.
366 Associated Press, April 6, 1999
367 Ibid.
368 New York Times, Oct. 11, 1998
369 Casper (WY) Star-Tribune, Oct. 17, 1998
370 Associated Press, Dec. 3, 1998
371 Ibid.
372 Los Angeles Times, March 24, 1999
373 Philadelphia Inquirer, Oct. 25, 1999
374 USA Today, March 24, 1999
375 Los Angeles Times, April 6, 1999
376 Ibid.
377 Associated Press, March 25, 1999
378 Ibid.
379 Ibid.
380 Ibid.
381 Philadelphia Inquirer, Oct. 25, 1999

382 Associated Press, March 25, 1999
383 Los Angeles Times, April 6, 1999
384 Associated Press, April 6, 1999
385 Los Angeles Times, April 6, 1999
386 Associated Press, April 6, 1999
387 Los Angeles Times, April 6, 1999]
388 Associated Press, April 6, 1999
389 Ibid.
390 Los Angeles Times, March 24, 1999
391 Gannett News Service, Oct. 11, 1999
392 Ibid.
393 Casper (WY) Star-Tribune, June 25, 1999
394 Ibid.
395 Ibid.
396 Ibid.
397 Ibid.
398 Philadelphia Inquirer, Oct. 25, 1999
399 Ibid.
400 Ibid.
401 Casper (WY) Star-Tribune, Oct. 26, 1999
402 Ibid.
403 Ibid.
404 Ibid.
405 Casper (WY) Star-Tribune, Oct. 27, 1999
406 Casper (WY) Star-Tribune, Oct. 28, 1999
407 Ibid.
408 Casper (WY) Star-Tribune, Nov. 2, 1999
409 Casper (WY) Star-Tribune, Oct. 29, 1999
410 Ibid.
411 Ibid.
412 Ibid.
413 Casper (WT) Star-Tribune, Nov. 2, 1999
414 Associated Press, Nov. 3, 1999
415 Ibid.
416 Casper (WY) Star-Tribune, Nov. 5, 1999
417 Shepard, Judy. (2009). *The Meaning of Matthew: My Son's Murder in Laramie, and a World Transformed.* New York: Hudson Street Press/Penguin Group.
418 Ibid.
419 Casper (WY) Star-Tribune, Nov. 5, 1999
420 Los Angeles Times, April 6, 1999
421 Associated Press, Sept. 8, 1904
422 Ibid.
423 Ibid.

424 Ibid.
425 Ibid.
426 Ibid.
427 Ibid.
428 Ibid.
429 Rochester (NY) Democrat & Chronicle, Sept. 9, 1904
430 Ibid.
431 Associated Press, Sept. 15, 1904
432 Associated Press, Sept. 16, 1904
433 Ibid.
434 Charlotte (NC) Observer, Sept. 20, 1904
435 Associated Press, Sept. 22-23, 1904; Associated Press, Sept. 26, 1904
436 "Many Indicted: Federal Grand Jury Takes up the Lynching Question." (1904, Oct. 27).
437 Associated Press, Feb, 6, 1913
438 Ibid.
439 Associated Press, Feb. 7, 1913
440 Associated Press, Feb, 6, 1913
441 Ibid.
442 Associated Press, Feb. 7, 1913
443 Ibid.
444 Atlanta Constitution, Feb. 9, 1913
445 Ibid.
446 Associated Press, Feb. 7, 1913
447 Associated Press, Feb. 8, 1913
448 Jackson Daily News, Feb. 9, 1913
449 Ibid.
450 Ibid.
451 Associated Press, Feb. 9, 1913
452 Jackson Daily News, Feb. 9, 1913
453 Vicksburg Evening Press, Feb. 10, 1913
454 Associated Press, Feb. 9, 1913
455 Associated Press, Aug. 3, 1920
456 Ibid.
457 Associated Press, Aug. 2, 1920
458 Marshall (TX) News Messenger, Aug. 4, 1920
459 Famous Trees of Texas. "Center Hanging Oak." Texas A&M University. Retrieved online at: http://texasforestservice.tamu.edu/websites/FamousTreesOfTexas/TreeLayout.aspx?pageid=15845
460 D'Souza, Dilip. (2010). "Today in Texas History." Retrieved online at: http://blog.chron.com/txpotomac/2010/08/today-in-texas-history-teenage-boy-lynched-in-center/
461 Associated Press, May 21, 1928

462 Ibid.
463 Waco (TX) News-Tribune, May 22, 1928
464 Associated Press, July 5, 2015
465 Lexington History Museum. "Lockett Trial/Hardeman Murder."
466 Associated Press, Feb. 9, 1920
467 United Press International, Feb. 5, 1920
468 Associated Press, Feb. 9, 1920
469 Ibid.
470 Lexington History Museum. "Lockett Trial/Hardeman Murder."
471 Associated Press, Feb. 9, 1920
472 Lexington History Museum. "Lockett Trial/Hardeman Murder."
473 Associated Press, Feb. 10, 1920
474 Lexington Herald-Leader, June 15, 2014
475 United Press International, Feb. 9, 1920
476 Associated Press, Feb. 9, 1920
477 Associated Press, Feb. 10, 1920
478 Ibid.
479 Associated Press, March 8, 1920
480 Ibid.
481 Associated Press, March 11, 1920
482 Ibid.
483 Lexington Herald-Leader, June 15, 2014=
484 Associated Press, Aug. 8, 1930
485 Ibid.
486 Ibid.
487 Associated Press, Dec. 31, 1930
488 Associated Press, Aug. 8, 1930
489 Ibid.
490 Kokomo Tribune, Aug. 8, 1930
491 Associated Press, Aug. 8, 1930
492 Ibid.
493 Ibid.
494 Kokomo Tribune, Aug. 8, 1930
495 Associated Press, Aug. 8, 1930
496 Kokomo Tribune, Aug. 8, 1930
497 Associated Press, Aug. 8, 1930
498 Associated Press, Aug. 9, 1930
499 Ibid.
500 Associated Press, Aug. 8, 1930
501 Associated Press, Aug. 9, 1930
502 Ibid.
503 Marion Chronicle, Aug. 8, 1930
504 Associated Press, Aug. 9, 1930
505 Indianapolis Star, Nov. 9, 1930

506 Indianapolis Star, Oct. 27, 1931
507 Madison, James H. (2001). *A Lynching in the Heartland: Race and Memory in America*. New York: Palgrave MacMillan.
508 Indianapolis Star, Nov. 24, 2001
509 New York Times, June 12, 2006; Washington Post, June 13, 2006
510 *Lynchings and What They Mean.* (1931). A Report of the Southern Commission on the Study of Lynching: Atlanta, Ga.
511 Lubbock (TX) Morning Avalanche, May 10, 1930
512 Ibid.
513 Ibid.
514 Ibid.
515 Ibid.
516 Ibid.
517 Associated Press, May 12, 1930
518 Ibid.
519 Kerrville (TX) Times, May 15, 1930
520 Ibid.
521 Ibid.
522 Associated Press, May 18, 1930; United Press, May 19, 1930
523 United Press, May 19, 1930; Associated Press, Aug. 6, 1930
524 Associated Press, May 26, 1930
525 http://www.texasescapes.com/CentralTexasTownsNorth/Sherman-Texas-Grayson-County-Courthouse.htm#1876
526 Baltimore Sun, Dec. 6, 1931
527 Ibid.
528 Ibid.
529 Washington Post, July 20, 2015
530 Baltimore Sun, Dec. 4, 1931
531 Washington Post, July 20, 2015
532 Baltimore Sun, Dec. 6, 1931
533 Baltimore Sun, Dec. 4, 1931
534 Ibid.
535 Washington Post, July 20, 2015
536 Salisbury Daily Times, Dec. 5, 1931
537 Ibid.
538 Baltimore Sun, Dec. 4, 1931
539 Baltimore Sun, Dec. 6, 1931]
540 Salisbury Daily Times, Dec. 5, 1931
541 Salisbury Daily Times, March 18, 1932
542 Baltimore Sun, March 19, 1932
543 Nashville Tennessean, Dec. 20, 1934
544 Associated Press, Dec. 19, 1934
545 Nashville Tennessean, Dec. 20, 1934
546 Ibid.

547 Ibid.
548 Ibid.
549 Ibid.
550 Ibid.
551 Ibid.
552 Associated Press, Dec. 22, 1934
553 Nashville Tennessean, Dec. 11, 1935
554 Associated Press, May 22, 1936
555 United Press, May 22, 1936
556 Associated Press, May 22, 1936
557 United Press, May 22, 1936
558 Nashville Tennessean, Jan. 8, 1935
559 Associated Press, May 4, 1935
560 Margolick, David. (2001). *Strange Fruit: The Biography of a Song.* New York: HarperCollins Publishers, Inc.
561 Smead, Howard. (1986). *Blood Justice: The Lynching of Mack Charles Parker.* New York: Oxford University Press.
562 Associated Press, April 25, 1959
563 Ibid.
564 Ibid.
565 Ibid.
566 Jackson (MS) Daily News, April 26, 1959
567 United Press International, April 27, 1959
568 Jackson (MS) Daily News, April 26, 1959
569 Jackson (MS) Clarion-Ledger, April 27, 1959
570 Associated Press, April 27, 1959; Jackson (MS) Clarion-Ledger, April 28, 1959
571 Associated Press, April 27, 1959
572 Ibid.
573 Ibid.
574 Associated Press, April 29, 1959
575 Associated Press, May 6, 1959
576 Ibid.
577 Ibid.
578 Baltimore (MD) Afro-American, May 16, 1959
579 Ibid.
580 Ibid.
581 Ibid.
582 Ibid.
583 Ibid.
584 Ibid.
585 Ibid.
586 Smead, Howard. (1986). *Blood Justice: The Lynching of Mack Charles Parker.* New York: Oxford University Press.